DATE DUE		

THE NEW YORK SUBWAYS

LESLEY A. DuTEMPLE

Lerner Publications Company
Minneapolis

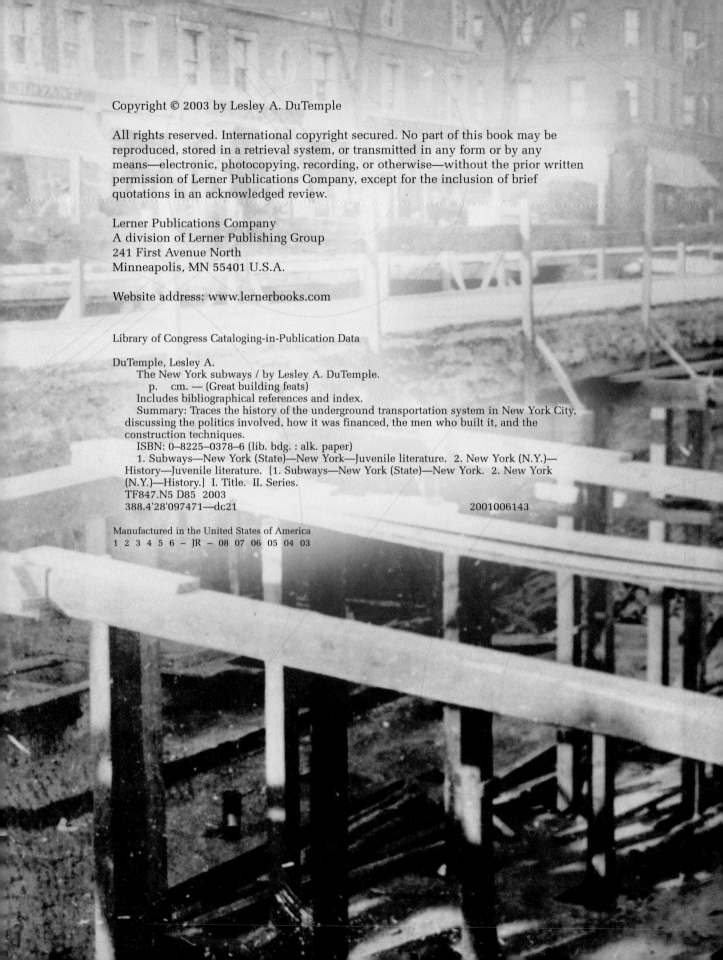

Lerner Publications Company
A division of Lerner Publishing Group
241 First Avenue North
Minneapolis, MN 55401 U.S.A.

Website address: www.lernerbooks.com

Library of Congress Cataloging-in-Publication Data

DuTemple, Lesley A.
      The New York subways / by Lesley A. DuTemple.
          p.   cm. — (Great building feats)
      Includes bibliographical references and index.
      Summary: Traces the history of the underground transportation system in New York City, discussing the politics involved, how it was financed, the men who built it, and the construction techniques.
      ISBN: 0–8225–0378–6 (lib. bdg. : alk. paper)
      1. Subways—New York (State)—New York—Juvenile literature. 2. New York (N.Y.)—History—Juvenile literature. [1. Subways—New York (State)—New York. 2. New York (N.Y.)—History.] I. Title. II. Series.
      TF847.N5 D85 2003
      388.4'28'097471—dc21   2001006143

Manufactured in the United States of America
1 2 3 4 5 6 – JR – 08 07 06 05 04 03

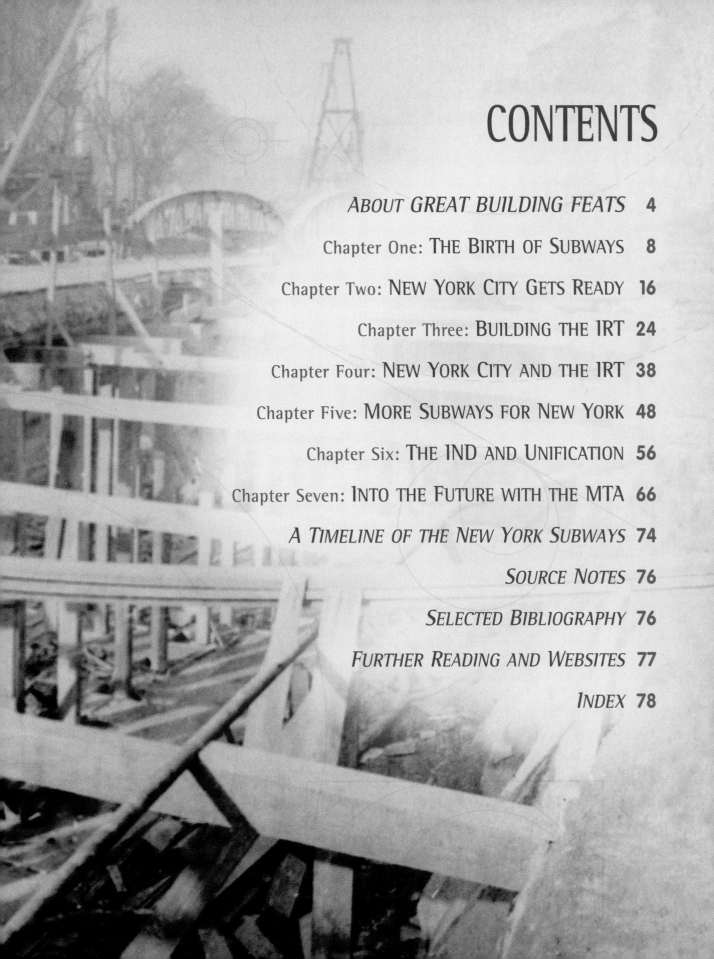

CONTENTS

ABOUT GREAT BUILDING FEATS

HUMANS HAVE LONG SOUGHT to make their mark on the world. From the ancient Great Wall of China to the ultramodern Channel Tunnel linking Britain and France, grand stuctures reveal how people have tried to express themselves and better their lives.

Great structures have served a number of purposes. Sometimes they met a practical need. For example, the New York subway system made getting around a huge city easier. Other structures reflected spiritual beliefs. The Pantheon in Rome, Italy, was created as a temple to Roman gods and later became a Catholic church. Sometimes we can only guess at the story behind a structure. The purpose of Stonehenge in England eludes us and perhaps always will.

New York subways carry millions of people all over the city.

This book is one in a series called Great Building Feats. Each book in the series takes a close look at some of the most amazing building feats around the world. Each of them posed a unique set of engineering and geographical problems. In many cases, these problems seemed nearly insurmountable when construction began.

More than a compilation of facts, the Great Building Feats series not only describes how each structure was built but also why. Each project called forth the best minds of its time. Many people invested their all in the outcome. Their lives are as much a part of the structure as the earth and stone used in the construction. Finally, each structure in the Great Building Feats series remains a dynamic feature of the modern world, still amazing users and viewers and historians.

THE NEW YORK SUBWAY SYSTEM

Railroads began to be built in the late 1700s, but the idea of putting them underground didn't occur to anyone until the mid-1800s. The New York subway system was an amazing engineering feat when it was finally constructed early in the twentieth century.

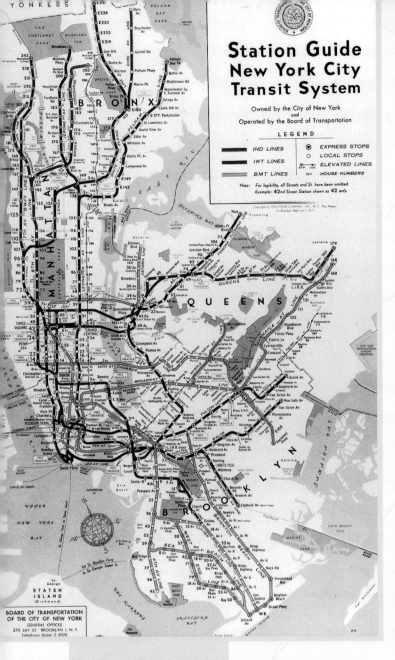

The New York subway system carries passengers to and from Manhattan, Brooklyn, Queens, and the Bronx.

Since the subway opened in October 1904, New Yorkers have used it enthusiastically, and in 2000, nearly 4.3 million New Yorkers rode it every weekday. The system set the world record for passengers transported in a single day on December 23, 1946: 8,772,244 passengers.

The New York subways were not the first subways to be constructed. Built almost entirely by manual labor, they burrowed through some of the most daunting geography of American cities of the East Coast.

Earlier European subways had been constructed to move people within large, already developed cities. But the New York subways were deliberately designed to open up vast tracts of undeveloped land. They created new neighborhoods and helped turn a cramped and crowded immigrant city into a sprawling metropolis. For many years, New Yorkers could explore the entire city for a nickel fare.

The first section of subway system was built and operated by a private company, because the government of New York City didn't want to take on the project. In addition, the general public didn't trust their city government to do it honestly. But the city government soon realized that there needed to be more public control of the system to make sure that private operators didn't have a free hand in operating the lines. The final section of subway ended up being built and operated entirely by the city, and ultimately, the city of New York owned and operated the entire system. Politics and financial dealings caused the subway to go from being a clean, safe, fast form of transportation—the pride of New York City—to a filthy, poorly maintained, crime-ridden system. Only since the 1980s has New York begun to work on rebuilding its subway system once again.

In 1982 the federal, city, and state governments dedicated more than $24 million dollars to the renovation of New York City's transit system. Most of its stations and tracks have been repaired and upgraded. All lines have new graffiti-proof cars. As the New York subway system celebrates its one-hundredth birthday, this great building feat is once again the pride of New York City.

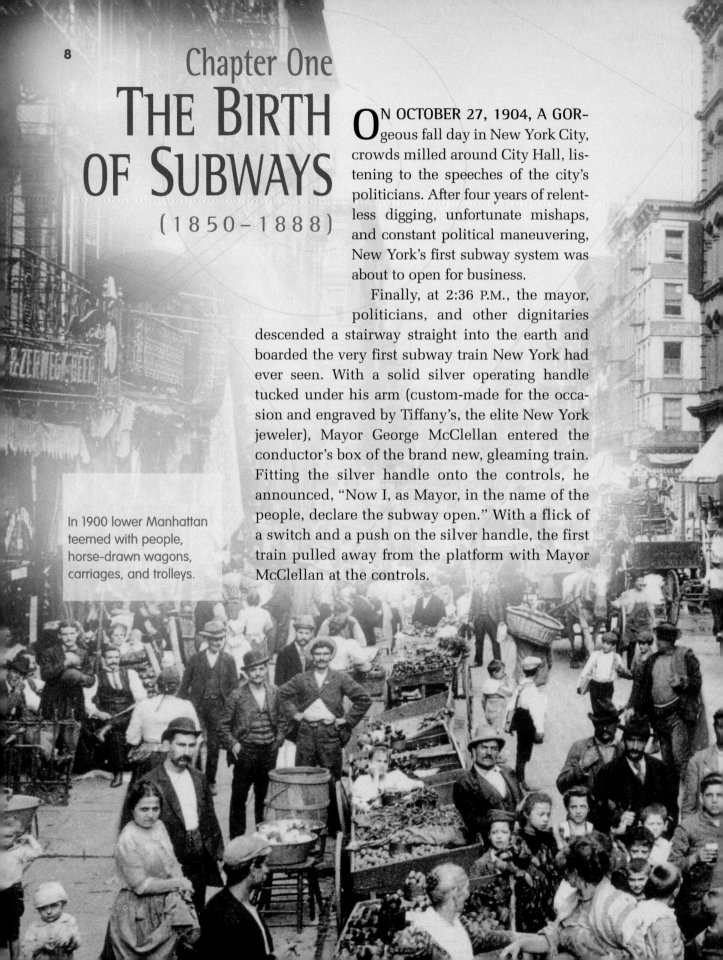

Chapter One
THE BIRTH OF SUBWAYS
(1850–1888)

ON OCTOBER 27, 1904, A GORgeous fall day in New York City, crowds milled around City Hall, listening to the speeches of the city's politicians. After four years of relentless digging, unfortunate mishaps, and constant political maneuvering, New York's first subway system was about to open for business.

Finally, at 2:36 P.M., the mayor, politicians, and other dignitaries descended a stairway straight into the earth and boarded the very first subway train New York had ever seen. With a solid silver operating handle tucked under his arm (custom-made for the occasion and engraved by Tiffany's, the elite New York jeweler), Mayor George McClellan entered the conductor's box of the brand new, gleaming train. Fitting the silver handle onto the controls, he announced, "Now I, as Mayor, in the name of the people, declare the subway open." With a flick of a switch and a push on the silver handle, the first train pulled away from the platform with Mayor McClellan at the controls.

In 1900 lower Manhattan teemed with people, horse-drawn wagons, carriages, and trolleys.

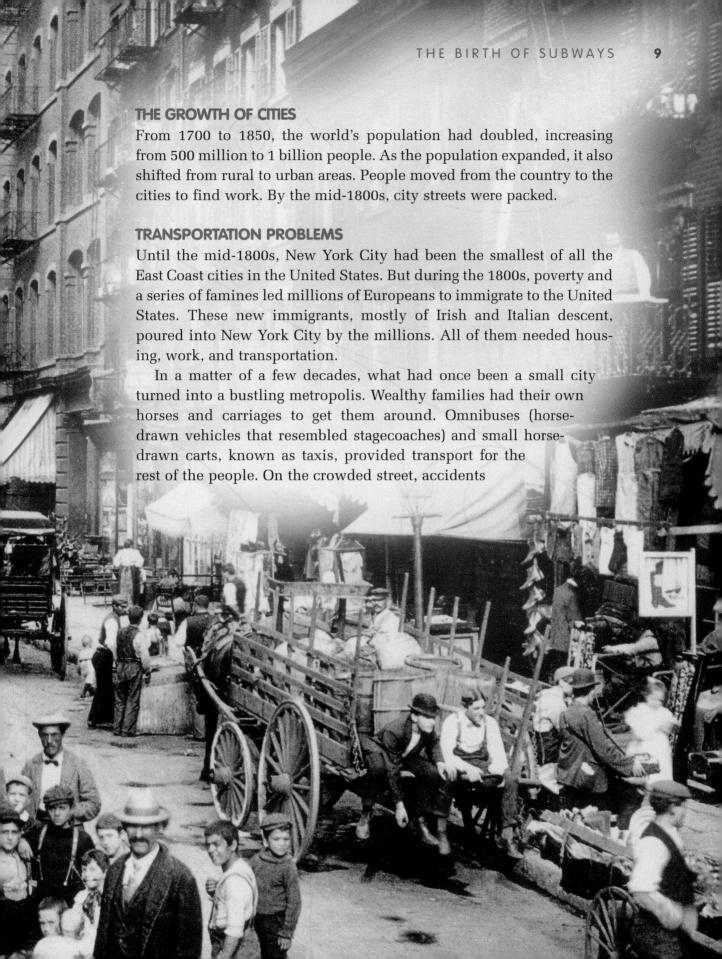

THE GROWTH OF CITIES

From 1700 to 1850, the world's population had doubled, increasing from 500 million to 1 billion people. As the population expanded, it also shifted from rural to urban areas. People moved from the country to the cities to find work. By the mid-1800s, city streets were packed.

TRANSPORTATION PROBLEMS

Until the mid-1800s, New York City had been the smallest of all the East Coast cities in the United States. But during the 1800s, poverty and a series of famines led millions of Europeans to immigrate to the United States. These new immigrants, mostly of Irish and Italian descent, poured into New York City by the millions. All of them needed housing, work, and transportation.

In a matter of a few decades, what had once been a small city turned into a bustling metropolis. Wealthy families had their own horses and carriages to get them around. Omnibuses (horse-drawn vehicles that resembled stagecoaches) and small horse-drawn carts, known as taxis, provided transport for the rest of the people. On the crowded street, accidents

BOSS TWEED AND TAMMANY HALL

In the mid-1800s, many large American cities were controlled by corrupt politicians. New York might have been the most corrupt of all, thanks in large part to one man—William Marcy Tweed, *below*, commonly referred to as Boss Tweed.

Tweed was Commissioner of Public Works. From his office in Tammany Hall (the building where New York City's Democratic Party was housed), he collected bribes in the form of fees from anybody who had anything to do with transportation in New York City. He controlled all licensing, and to get a license, you had to pay him personally. Tweed also controlled all construction in New York City. He and his henchmen stole millions of dollars from the city by demanding payoffs from contractors and taking a cut of inflated construction costs.

In 1871 the *New York Times* published several articles about Tweed's crooked dealings. The public outcry that followed forced Tweed to resign in 1872. The people of New York remained suspicious of all politicians for decades to come.

were daily occurrences. Horses reared and shied, axles and wheels broke, and carriages crashed. It seemed as if policemen spent more time separating fighting drivers than directing traffic.

RAILROADS IN THE AIR

The first solution to New York City's traffic problems was an elevated railroad that was called an el. Charles Harvey conceived of the first el in the 1860s, designing it to run on tracks above the street. It was an ingenious idea but one that many people, especially New York City's politicians, didn't think would work.

That skepticism turned out to be a good thing because New York's government was very corrupt in the 1860s. William "Boss" Tweed ran things in New York City. He personally collected bribes from every omnibus and horse cart operator who wanted to work in the city. Tweed had opposed other transportation solutions (including the plans for the first subway in 1864) simply because other forms of transportation would have competed with his horse traffic business. Because Tweed didn't take Harvey's elevated railroad seriously, he didn't oppose it.

In July, 1867, Harvey started

Harvey's elevated railroad moved traffic off the street to overhead tracks.

work on his West Side & Yonkers Patent Railway. The railroad followed the city's streets atop iron supports about 25 feet (8 meters) above ground, or about as high as a two-story building.

Harvey's elevated railway proved the skeptics wrong, especially Boss Tweed. Although the el spewed smoke and soot all over people on the streets below and added to the already deafening noise level, the people of New York City used it. By 1876 the el was carrying 340,000 passengers each year. More lines were added, and in 1883 a cable-car system was built to cross the Brooklyn Bridge.

By the 1880s, els and horse-drawn trolley cars, which traveled on street-level tracks, crisscrossed most of Manhattan and Brooklyn (two main boroughs, or sections, of New York City). But it still wasn't enough. In 1888 Mayor Abram Hewitt proposed a solution to New York City's transportation mess— build a subway. He felt that a subway system financed by the city and operated by a private company was the best solution. Speaking in 1901, he said, "It was evident to me that underground rapid transit could not be secured by the investment of private capital, but in some way or other its construction was dependent upon ... the credit of the City of New York."

THE FIRST SUBWAY

The idea of putting a transportation system underground wasn't new. London, England, had been operating a subway since 1863. An immediate success, it carried forty thousand passengers on its first day of operation. (Londoners refer to their subway as the Underground or the tube, rather than the subway.)

London's original Underground was 3 miles (5 km) long and primarily constructed by the cut-and-cover method. In cut-and-cover construction, a large trench, 20 to 30 feet (6 to 9 m) deep, is dug along the route, and a railroad is built in the bottom of the trench. The width of the trench depends on how many sets of tracks will run in it.

When the railroad construction is complete, the trench is roofed with steel beams and covered. Then the street is put back in place on top. Although traffic and businesses are disrupted during cut-and-cover construction, this method is faster, cheaper, and easier than any other. Most subways are still constructed this way.

NEW YORK BASICS

Manhattan is an island 13 miles (21 kilometers) long and 2 miles (3 km) across. It is separated from New Jersey by the Hudson River. The other boroughs of New York City—the Bronx, Queens, Brooklyn, and Staten Island—are separated from Manhattan by the Harlem River, the East River, and Upper New York Bay. The earliest settlers and most immigrants landed at the southern tip of Manhattan, and most business had developed there.

Small communities and farms were scattered throughout upper Manhattan and the outer boroughs of New York City. But they were far away from downtown jobs, or they were separated from them by water. Local horse and ferry transportation was too slow to make these outlying areas easily accessible to downtown workers. Because of this, most working people, including the newcomers, sought housing in lower Manhattan. By the 1880s, teeming slums crowded the southern tip of the island. Some neighborhoods were among the most densely populated areas in the world.

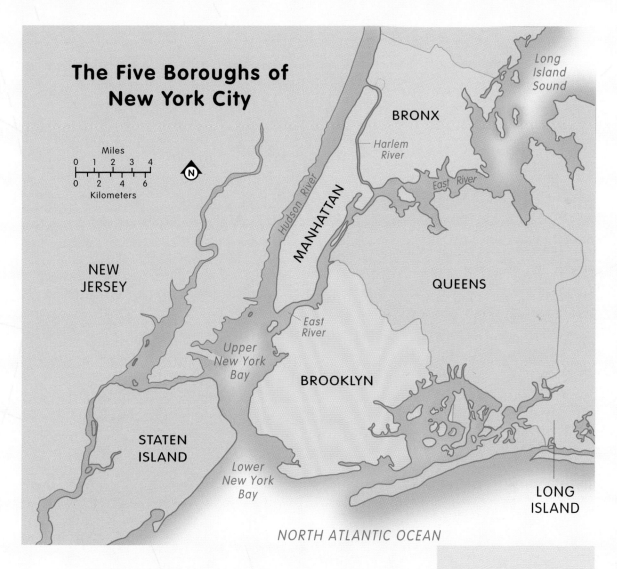

The Five Boroughs of New York City

Miles
0 1 2 3 4
0 2 4 6
Kilometers

N

Long Island Sound

BRONX

Harlem River

East River

Hudson River

MANHATTAN

NEW JERSEY

QUEENS

East River

Upper New York Bay

BROOKLYN

STATEN ISLAND

Lower New York Bay

LONG ISLAND

NORTH ATLANTIC OCEAN

Because London's Underground was literally a railroad that was underground and ran on coal-generated steam, it created a great deal of smoke and pollution. No matter how many ventilation openings to ground level were created, the smoke remained trapped in the underground tunnels. Many Londoners preferred to stick to cleaner aboveground transportation.

By the 1880s, Prague (in the modern-day Czech Republic) had a subway, too. An inventor had figured out how to use electricity to power streetcars.

The city of New York is made up of five boroughs separated by rivers and Upper and Lower New York Bay.

THE SECRET SUBWAY

Thirty years before work started on the New York subway system, a secret subway ran under the streets of Manhattan. It was created by Alfred E. Beach, an engineer, inventor, and successful publisher (his magazine, *Scientific American,* is still going strong), who was fascinated by underground transit systems. He decided to build an underground tunnel in which a subway car would be moved, not by a steam or electric engine, but by a powerful blast of air.

Building anything in New York meant getting construction permits—which meant paying Boss Tweed. Beach didn't want to have to bribe Tweed, and he didn't want Tweed to profit from his subway system. To keep his project secret, he filed a false permit requesting to build two small pneumatic, or air-powered, tubes under Broadway to transport mail between buildings.

In 1869 Beach rented the cellar of a clothing store on Broadway and had his workers start digging. All the digging was done in secret, often at night, since Beach didn't want anyone to discover his real plan until it was finished. Beach spent $350,000 of his own money to build the 312-foot-long (95 m) subway line and its two stations. When everything was ready, he invited city officials, newspaper reporters, and the general public to a grand opening of his subway on February 26, 1870.

People were stunned by Beach's accomplishment. The tunnel was lined with brick. The subway car was roomy and lavishly decorated. A giant fan propelled the car forward smoothly. The waiting room in one of the stations boasted a grand piano, an aquarium, and a bubbling fountain. Everyone who rode Beach's sample subway was impressed with its speed, cleanliness, and beauty.

Having managed to build and publicize his subway without paying Tweed, Beach hoped to build 5 more miles (8 m) of subway tunnels. He asked the state legislature for a subway charter, but Governor John Thompson Hoffman, a friend of Tweed, turned him down.

A few years later, Beach closed the subway line, and it was forgotten as the city grew over it. In 1912, nearly forty years later, workers excavating for a new Broadway subway line broke through the old tunnel wall. Everything was still intact, including a single subway car sitting on the tracks.

Electricity rapidly became the accepted method of powering transportation. The subways of Prague, Budapest (in Hungary), and Boston ran cleaner than the London Underground, because they used electricity to power the trains.

A SUBWAY FOR NEW YORK CITY

When Mayor Hewitt proposed a subway as the answer to New York City's transportation problems in 1888, he was aware of the earlier subways. He was convinced that New York City could take advantage of new construction methods, as well as learn from the mistakes other subway builders had made. But it would be another twelve years full of wrangling and false starts before construction would begin.

In 1870 Alfred E. Beach secretly built a short subway tunnel with one car under Broadway.

Chapter Two
NEW YORK CITY GETS READY
(1888–1900)

ON JANUARY 31, 1888, ABRAM Hewitt delivered his subway proposal to New York City's aldermen, or elected officials. People immediately began referring to the straightforward and simple plan as the Hewitt Formula.

The Hewitt Formula called for the city to arrange financing for and to retain ownership of a subway to be constructed beneath the streets of New York City. The city would select a company that would build the subway and then manage it for profit.

The Board of Rapid Transit Railroad Commissioners and August Belmont sign the contracts for the first subway line in New York.

The construction company would have to provide the funds for the purchase of equipment. The city would arrange most of the financing since no private company could raise the $30 million necessary.

When the subway was completed, the construction company would essentially own the system for the fifty-year term of the contract. The company would only have to make an annual payment to the city based on profits.

It took four years for Hewitt's proposal to work its way through the city government and the New York state legislature. But finally, in 1892, a subway commission was in place and ready to receive bids for the right to build the subway they had designed. Not one bid was submitted. The project was so large and the cost of construction so uncertain, no group was willing to assume the financial risk. Greatly disappointed, the subway commission was dissolved.

WILLIAM BARCLAY PARSONS

William Barclay Parsons, *below*, came from an old New York family. His colonial ancestors had fought for the British during the Revolutionary War, and the family still had strong ties to England. Parsons, born in 1859, spent much of his youth in England being privately educated. He returned to New York in 1875 to attend Columbia University, where he earned a degree in civil engineering.

Parsons was hired as chief engineer by a group of businessmen interested in building a subway in New York City. The company went bankrupt, but Parsons was hooked on the idea of a subway for New York.

On his own, he planned the best route for a subway and how to build it. He exploited his family's social connections and developed a friendship with Mayor Hewitt and other subway promoters. When the Rapid Transit Commission came into being, Parsons was appointed its chief engineer.

At age thirty-five, Parsons assumed direct control over the building of a subway for New York. Parsons was known for his engineering abilities and fairness, and his workers respected him. First-rate engineers and miners flocked to the project simply because he was in charge.

THE RAPID TRANSIT COMMISSION

This might have seemed like the end, but Hewitt refused to abandon the idea of a subway. Working behind the scenes, he kept the project alive. In 1894 a new subway commission formed, called the Board of Rapid Transit Railroad Commissioners, or Rapid Transit Commission. The RTC, as it came to be known, was headed by William Barclay Parsons, a talented engineer. Parsons was charged with producing the basic design for a subway system, and he was determined to succeed.

It took several years for Parsons and the commission to work out the design and deal with financing issues. By November of 1899, the RTC was ready to accept bids again.

MCDONALD "ALMOST" OWNS A SUBWAY

The RTC received only two bids. With very little deliberation, they accepted John B. McDonald's bid to build a subway for $35 million, $5 million more than the estimated cost four years earlier.

McDonald was certainly qualified. He had worked on the Croton Dam, which supplied water to New York City, and on various railroad projects, including a portion of New York's main railroad, the New York Central. Since the subway would essentially be a railroad underground, this was a critical point with the commissioners. Perhaps most important, McDonald really believed in the subway project.

The city agreed to help raise most of the necessary financing, but McDonald still had to come up with $7 million on his own. In the end, he was unable to raise the money.

AUGUST BELMONT AND THE NEW YORK SUBWAY

McDonald ended up surrendering his contract to a wealthy banker named August Belmont. Belmont didn't have the engineering qualifications to build a subway, but he definitely had the money. He thought of the New York subway as an investment opportunity, convinced that it would create a handsome profit for him. He would build a subway for New York, but only if he solely operated it. He said he had been long attracted to the "splendid opportunities . . . for making a great deal of money out of schemes for improving . . . transportation. . . . " The contract that Belmont signed on February 21, 1900, required him to build the subway, provide the equipment, and operate it for fifty years. Belmont would use the city's money to build the subway, then finance all cars, signals, and other equipment on his own. The city of New York would provide a total of $36.5 million, $1.5 million of it earmarked for the purchase of land. The subway itself would be constructed underground, but the stations, especially the entrances, would be above ground. Belmont would have to purchase the land on which to build the stations.

August Belmont, a wealthy banker, considered the subway an excellent investment opportunity.

After signing the contract, Belmont immediately formed two companies: the Rapid Transit Subway Construction Company, which would handle all

AUGUST BELMONT

August Belmont was one of the wealthiest men in New York, but his father came from humble beginnings. August Schönberg started out as a floor sweeper for a bank owned by the wealthy Rothschild family in Germany. He rose through the ranks, and in 1837, he was sent to New York as the Rothschild's representative. In New York, he was able to amass a small fortune though financial dealings, though he continued to represent the Rothschilds.

Although Schönberg was wealthy, it was a time of rigid class structure and open anti-Semitism. Society people snubbed Schönberg because he was Jewish. Undeterred, Schönberg changed his name to Belmont, the French version of his German name. He became an Episcopalian and married into a prominent family. Soon, he was part of New York's social elite, and people forgot he was a German Jew.

His son, August Belmont, belonged to this privileged world from the moment of his birth in 1853. The wealth and social prestige his father had fought to obtain were taken for granted by the son. Reports indicate that the younger Belmont was arrogant, mean-spirited, pompous, and had a foul temper. He joined his father's bank in 1874 and inherited the entire operation sixteen years later, when he was thirty-seven years old.

Belmont owned seven houses and lived like a prince. Horses were his passion. In 1902 he built Belmont Race Track, which is still in existence. He had his own railcar, the *Mineola,* to take him to the track. His stables produced a horse that many view as the best Thoroughbred racehorse that ever lived: Man O' War.

construction, and the Interborough Rapid Transit Company (the IRT), which would operate the subway once it was finished. The first New York subway came to be known as the IRT. Belmont hired John B. McDonald as his chief building contractor.

WHERE WILL THE SUBWAY GO?

Belmont, with McDonald, was building the subway, but the Rapid Transit Commission, specifically William Barclay Parsons, still had control over the plan. By the time Belmont signed the contract, nearly every detail had already been worked out: the routes, the location and design of the stations, the method of construction, and the source of power. Parsons was even considering the design of the passenger cars. Belmont had to follow Parson's plans and answer to the RTC.

For the route, Parsons and the RTC had decided that the subway would run in a loop starting at City Hall, at the southern end of Manhattan. After leaving City Hall, the subway would head up the east side of Manhattan to 42nd Street. Then it would turn west to Broadway and continue north to 145th Street and on into the Bronx, ending at 242nd Street.

All lines would run through underground tunnels. A little over half of the construction would be by the cut-and-cover method. Some sections would have to be tunneled through bedrock and beneath the East River. Where the route passed through a fourteen-block depression known as Manhattan Valley, the tracks would be elevated. Belmont agreed to build 21 miles (34 km) of track, 16 (26 km) of them underground and 5 of them (8 km) elevated.

JOHN B. MCDONALD

John B. McDonald, *below,* had every qualification needed to build the New York subway, ex-cept the ability to raise sufficient money. When he submitted his bid to the RTC, he already had more than thirty years of construction experience under his belt.

McDonald was born in Cork, Ireland, in 1844, and his family immigrated to New York when he was only three years old. To help his struggling family get by, McDonald quit school when he was young and went to work as a timekeeper on a reservoir project.

After working as a low-level supervisor on several other projects, he was hired by the company building a railroad tunnel under Park Avenue in New York City for Cornelius Vanderbilt, one of the weal-thiest men in the world. Based on his performance on that job, McDonald began to get railroad construction contracts all over eastern North America.

McDonald was known for managing his workers and getting his jobs finished in time and within budget. His workers liked and respected him. He also enjoyed a warm relationship with the politicians in Tammany Hall, since many of them, like him, were of Irish descent.

William Parsons had created his subway plan to accomplish two objectives: First, move people about *in* crowded Man hattan; second, get them *out* of crowded Manhattan. In the Bronx, the subway ended in a cow pasture. By extending the subway into an undeveloped area, the RTC was hoping to encourage development and to relieve some of the congestion downtown.

There was no easy way to get into Manhattan from the Bronx, which was across the Harlem River. Without transportation to and from work, people essentially had to live within walking distance of their jobs. Before the subway was built, it took about an hour and a half to get into Manhattan by horse trolley and ferry— even though downtown Manhattan was only a few miles away.

Before there were subways, horse trolleys— carriages on tracks that were pulled by teams of horses—carried workers into downtown Manhattan.

HUNGARIAN STATIONS

Parsons's subway plan grew out of his thorough study of every other subway system in the world. The subway in Budapest, Hungary, impressed him the most. He followed the Budapest plan for New York City, right down to the subterranean stations and street-level entrance kiosks. Forty-nine stations were planned for the first section of the subway. At street level, each station had an entrance kiosk to keep out rain and snow. The kiosks were made of cast iron and glass, with a domed roof.

Concrete stairways brought passengers down from the street level to the subway platforms. Because the subway tunnels were constructed close to the surface (the cut-and-cover method usually only dug down about 30 feet, or 9 m), only two stations were deep enough to require elevators.

NO SOOT, NO SMOKE

Parsons was determined to avoid the filth and pollution he'd seen in the London Underground. A few years earlier, London had opened up two new routes powered by electricity. Although there were problems with both lines (they were very small, very slow, and very noisy), they were much cleaner than the lines powered by steam engines.

The electric routes of the London Underground were also cheaper to operate, and they even generated a small profit for the city of London. Parsons wanted a clean subway, and he liked the idea that an electric subway might be profitable. Electric power had been around for several decades, but it had only been in use as a source of transportation power for about ten years. To base the entire subway system of a huge city on a relatively untried power source was a risky decision.

Running an entire subway system took more power than lighting a few street lamps or homes. Powering the trains wouldn't be the only drain on the power supply either. Thousands of electric lights also would be needed for illumination, since everything was underground. The city would need to build a new power plant exclusively for the subway. Building a power plant wasn't part of Belmont's job. The city would build it, making sure that it was ready by the time the subway was open for business. With the routes planned out, the construction method determined, and a construction company in place, the only thing left to do was start digging.

Chapter Three
BUILDING THE IRT
(1900–1904)

O N MARCH 24, 1900, BARELY a month after Belmont won the subway bid, more than twenty-five thousand people gathered in the small park across from New York's City Hall to commemorate the start of construction of the New York subway system. Cannons boomed, church bells tolled, and fireworks exploded in the air. The famous bandleader John Philip Sousa led his band through several stirring musical numbers. Two days later, the workers started to dig.

New York dignitaries gathered across from City Hall for the groundbreaking ceremony, March 24, 1900.

SAND, ROCKS, VALLEYS, AND HILLS

Digging a subway by hand on the island of Manhattan turned out to be more difficult than Belmont, Parsons, and the RTC had ever imagined. The island of Manhattan is an irregular rectangle that tapers slightly at the northern end. Even though Manhattan Island is not very big, its geology is rugged, forbidding, and full of surprises.

The island can be roughly divided into three geographical zones. The first zone, at the southern end of the island (where the subway started), is level, with no unusual features. By 1900 most of this area had long been built over, and the original hills and valleys had been flattened.

WHO BUILT THE NEW YORK SUBWAY?

More than 7,700 workers were employed in building the subway. Most of these men were Irish and Italian immigrants, *below*. There also were some German and Greek immigrants, as well as some African Americans.

Most were unskilled laborers who earned $2.00 to $2.25 a day. These were the people who dug, shoveled dirt, cleared rocks, and pounded the railway lines together. Workers who performed tasks requiring more skill, such as measuring and pouring concrete or laying out the rail routes, earned $2.50 a day.

Skilled miners did all the tunnel construction. The project attracted miners from all over the world. They came from Colorado in the United States, from South Africa, Wales, Ireland, Canada, and Scandinavia just to work on the New York subway. Miners received $3.75 a day. They referred to the subway as "the mine," to distinguish themselves from the other workers.

All subway workers led rough lives. The hours were long and hard, the work dangerous. Most lived in dirty, cramped boardinghouses— with or without their families. None had health or accident insurance. When one of them was injured, few people noticed.

The second geographical zone, at the middle of the island, is rougher, with steep hills and rocky outcroppings. But like the southern zone, by 1900 the terrain of the middle zone had long been covered with buildings, erasing many of its hills and valleys.

The third geographical zone, at the northern end of the island, was the most difficult for subway construction. It was dominated by high ridges, low valleys, rocky outcroppings, and two broad plains. In 1900, when subway construction began, very little of the third zone had been built on, and subway workers had to deal with all its geographical complexity.

The rock underlying most of the island is known as Manhattan schist. It is extremely hard and very difficult to cut through. But the schist also contains pockets of crumbling, decaying rock. Because the composition of Manhattan schist is so unpredictable, it can be dangerous to work with.

To make matters more difficult, the Manhattan schist wasn't always at the same level. In some places, it was 10 feet (3 m) below the surface, while in others it was 50 (15 m). Parsons decided to dig the subway trench only 15 to 20 feet (4.5 to 6 m) below the surface to minimize the amount of schist workers would have to excavate.

DIGGING THROUGH AN OBSTACLE COURSE

No matter where the subway was being built, the first step was to clear a street of traffic and dig a trench as wide as the street and about 20 feet (6 m) deep. Later on, workers built temporary wooden bridges over the trench or entirely covered it with wood, so as not to disrupt traffic and business. But in the beginning, most of the trenches were left open, which meant that the whole street closed down during construction.

The ground beneath the streets of Manhattan was full of sewer pipes, water mains, electrical conduits, pneumatic mail tubes, and other human-made obstacles. Most of these pipes had been laid over the years

Most of the excavation for the first subways was done by hand. Workers shoveled dirt and rocks into wheelbarrows and dumped the load into horse-drawn carts.

without any plan. They twisted about each other in a tangled maze. Many of the buildings in Manhattan had storage vaults that extended out from their foundations beneath the street, and these, too, had to be moved. Then, with so much of the street excavated, many of the buildings had to have their foundations propped up and reinforced while construction was going on.

In 1900 there was very little modern construction technology: no bulldozers, no tractors, no dump trucks, and only a few mechanical shovels. Almost all the work on the IRT section of the New York subway was done by humans using hand tools. Workers shoveled dirt by hand, loaded it into wheelbarrows, and wheeled it up rickety wooden planks. The dirt was dumped into horse-drawn carts and hauled to the outskirts of the city.

Then the workers got down to the business of relocating, bypassing, or entirely rebuilding the pipes and conduits. The original sewers were of brick, which is very difficult to disassemble and relocate. It was like trying to move a giant jigsaw puzzle. Subway workers found drinking water pipes, encrusted with filth, actually running within the sewer pipes. Eventually, 45 miles (72 km) of new sewer, water, and other pipes were laid during the building of the New York subway system.

A RAILROAD IN A DITCH

Once the trench was the correct depth and width and free from obstacles, the workers poured a 4-inch (10 centimeter) slab of concrete over the bottom. This concrete floor provided a firm base upon which to lay the track. It also minimized seepage and flooding in the tunnel.

To build the sides of the subway tunnel, workers lined the dirt sides of the trench with large steel beams spaced 5 feet (1.5 m) apart. Then they erected a wooden wall about 12 inches (30 cm) away from the dirt wall of the trench. This served as a mold for the concrete. Workers next poured wet concrete into the space between the wooden wall and the dirt. When the concrete hardened, they removed the wood. The steel beams embedded in the thick concrete lined the tunnel. The beams ensured that the finished tunnel would be strong enough to support the weight of the street and traffic above when the subway was finished.

Once the concrete floor and the walls hardened, workers built a railroad in the trench. First they put a layer of crushed stone about 8 inches (20 cm) thick on top of the concrete floor. Then they laid the wooden cross-ties that held track about 2 feet (0.6 m) apart on top of the crushed stone. The steel tracks were placed on top of the wooden ties and bolted down.

DISCOVERIES AND HIDDEN TREASURES

Sewer pipes and conduits weren't the only things found by diggers beneath the streets of Manhattan. At the corner of Madison Avenue and 32nd Street, workers uncovered an old pond where early New Yorkers had once fished. At the corner of Mulberry and Baxter Streets, workers found a mineral spring once visited by people who believed it had curative powers. Although the pond and spring were both mentioned in historical records, both had long been covered over. These and the other underground springs that were found in the excavations had all become polluted.

Workers often came upon weapons, tools, and household items from the colonial period. There were long-forgotten chests of coins buried by early New Yorkers.

The most surprising find was the remains of the Dutch ship *Tiger*. The *Tiger* had burned and sunk in 1613. So much of the harbor had been filled in over the years, its remains were under earth, not under water. During the construction of the Dyckman Street station, workers found their oldest relic—the bones of a giant mastodon.

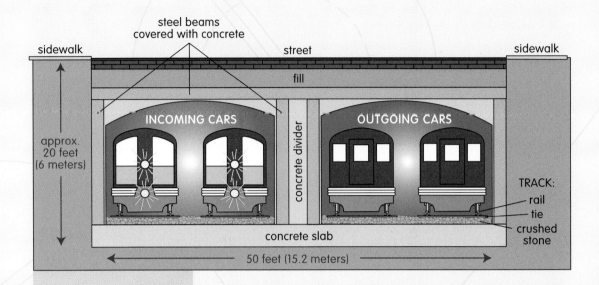

This cross-section drawing of a subway tunnel shows the steel beams and concrete walls, floor, and ceiling.

Two sets of tracks ran north, and two sets ran south. A dividing wall was added between the north and south tracks. Workers built guardrails at every curve to keep the trains from jumping the tracks.

Once a section of the subway was finished, the trench was roofed over and the workers moved on to the next section. To cover the subway tunnel, workers used the same technique they used to construct the walls. They built a wooden temporary roof, placed steel beams across it, and poured concrete. When the concrete was dry, they pulled away the wood, leaving a steel-reinforced concrete roof in place. More than half of the IRT was built in this cut-and-cover fashion, usually one or two city blocks at a time.

ELS AND TUNNELS

In many places, Manhattan was so hilly that following the contours of the land would have made the subway resemble an underground roller coaster. To keep it level, Belmont had to build elevated tracks across low areas and dig tunnels through hills.

Building elevated tracks for the subway wasn't particularly difficult. Workers just built bridges with railroad tracks on top of them, something the railroad industry had been doing for decades.

But tunneling was grueling and diffi- cult, and most transportation companies tried to avoid it. Most of the other subway systems in exis- tence in 1900 had been con- structed almost entirely by cut-and-cover. Some of London's Underground had been tunneled, but the tun- nels had gone through flat, stable soil, not through hills and Manhattan schist. New York's first subway system contained two rock tunnels: one in an area called Murray Hill and the other in upper Manhattan.

To create a tunnel, work- ers dug vertical shafts at each end of the proposed tunnel. They cleared a small space at the bottom of each shaft, drilled holes 7 feet (2 m) long into the rock, and packed them full of dynamite. After the dynamite had been deto- nated, workers crawled back down, cleared out the rubble, propped up the jagged sides of the tunnel with wood, and began the process all over again. This process continued until the two work crews met in the

WORKERS' WAGES

Unskilled laborers:
$2.00 to $2.25 per day

Slightly skilled workers:
$2.50 per day

Skilled miners:
$3.75 per day

middle. Once the tunnel was completely open, workers covered the rock with concrete or sometimes with sheets of iron and then laid down the tracks.

ACCIDENTS AND DISASTERS

McDonald's workers might go for weeks, even months without mishap. But disaster could strike at any time. The sides of a trench could collapse, injuring, trapping, or even killing workers. Or a wooden structure built to cover an open trench could give way. This usually happened because of the excessive weight of people, horses, and trolley cars on the temporary roadway covering the trench. One cave-in near Park Avenue caused such damage to property

Wooden roadways were built over the open trenches so that traffic could keep moving. Sometimes the wooden covering gave way, and trolleys, carriages, and pedestrians plunged into the trench.

THE VOODOO CONTRACTOR

Major Ira Shaler was thirty-eight years old when he started work as a subway construction supervisor. During the two years he worked on the subway, he encountered more bad luck than any other single person.

It was Shaler who was in charge of the section responsible for one of the worst dynamite disasters on the subway, the explosion that killed five people and injured more than one hundred eighty on January 28, 1902. Although an employee, Moses Epps, had started the fire, Shaler was ordered to appear in a New York courtroom, where he was indicted for manslaughter—a charge that carried a possible prison sentence.

Two months later, on the night of March 21, an enormous crack appeared in the roof of the Murray Hill tunnel—a section also under Shaler's supervision. Shaler got all his workers out before the tunnel caved in, but construction was delayed for weeks. Four Murray Hill homes were damaged beyond repair. August Belmont had to pay more than $100,000 to the owners.

By this time, Shaler was being referred to as the voodoo contractor, and three months later, his luck ran out completely. On June 17, Shaler and William Parsons were inspecting the Murray Hill tunnel. As they reached the western end, Parsons stopped and pointed to a rock protruding from the roof, warning that he thought it looked unstable. Shaler, insisting that it was just fine, stepped out from beneath the timber bracing for a closer look. Suddenly, the half-ton (454-kilogram) boulder broke loose and fell on Shaler. It broke his neck and paralyzed him. He died eleven days later. Parsons, who had stayed under the timber bracing, wasn't even scratched.

along the street that August Belmont decided to buy the entire block for $1 million rather than face the resulting lawsuits.

Working with dynamite was dangerous, whether to speed up cut-and-cover excavation or to blast out a rock tunnel. The mishandling of dynamite created problems for McDonald. On January 28, 1902, a worker named Moses Epps went into a storage shed to eat his lunch. To warm his hands, he lit a candle—only a few feet from 200 pounds (91 kilograms) of dynamite. Epps then left the shed to get something.

By the time Epps returned, the candle had fallen over, his lunch wrapper had caught fire, and the flames were spreading. Horrified, Epps rushed for a bucket of water and flung it on the flames. The fire continued to burn. Before he could return with a second bucket, the fire was out of control. Less than one minute later, the dynamite exploded, ripping through the work site and surrounding blocks.

Clouds of dust and debris filled the air. The Murray Hill Hotel was destroyed, Grand Central Terminal was defaced, and glass windows were shattered for several blocks around the site. Five people were killed and more than one hundred eighty were injured. The local hospital was so badly damaged, it was unable to help any of the accident

ARCHITECTS AND SUBWAY STATIONS

Right from the beginning, the Rapid Transit Commission wanted the subway stations to look nice. In its 1891 report, the commission specifically stated that every effort should be made "in the way of painting and decoration to give brightness and cheerfulness to the general effect."

Architects George Heins and Grant LaFarge were hired to decorate the interiors of the stations. The team was well known in New York, having already designed the Cathedral of Saint John the Divine and the New York Zoological Park.

There were forty-nine subway stations—thirty-seven underground and twelve aboveground. Heins and LaFarge used brick arches, leaded skylights, and chandeliers at the magnificent City Hall station. The others, though more modestly designed, still gleamed with oak and bronze ticket booths and with tile panels to help identify the stop.

At the Columbia University station, Heins and LaFarge incorporated the seal of the university into the walls. At Astor Place, the tile featured a beaver, to represent the fact that John Jacob Astor had made his fortune trading beaver and other furs. Columbus Circle had an embossed design of the *Santa Maria,* the flagship of Christopher Columbus's fleet.

Many of the stations renovated in the 1980s and 1990s display new mosaics and tilework in the spirit of Heins and LaFarge. These include the gilded Greek dancers at the Lincoln Center stop and a variety of animals, present and prehistoric, under the Museum of Natural History at the 79th Street station.

victims. Moses Epps, strangely enough, escaped with only a few cuts and bruises.

The single worst accident occurred in the upper Manhattan tunnel in October of 1903 and involved a combination of dynamite and a cave-in. For several weeks, workers had been blasting through Manhattan schist and having a bad time of it. The schist in this area was unstable and riddled with cracks. Only a few hundred feet remained. Even though the geology of the area demanded extra caution, the contractor, L. B. McCabe, was in a hurry to be done. He ordered three charges of dynamite to be set off every day instead of the usual two.

The City Hall station has colored brick arches, skylights, and chandeliers. This station is closed, but it can be seen on special tours.

Subway construction meant dirt and dust, impassable streets, and lost business.

On October 24, 1903, about fifteen minutes after one charge of dynamite had been detonated, twenty-two workers entered the tunnel to make sure it was safe. The supervisor, Timothy Sullivan, went first. Everything appeared stable, so he called out for the other workers to come. No one knew that there was an underground spring just behind the rock face, weakening the whole tunnel structure.

Moments later, a 300-ton (272-metric ton) boulder—44 feet (13 m) long and about 5 feet (1.5 m) wide—dropped from the roof, instantly killing six men and seriously injuring eight others. With the roof gone, more rocks came crashing down. All told, ten people were killed in the accident.

Generally speaking, accidents didn't really concern the RTC. In Parsons's report on the tunnel accident, he didn't even mention that the ten people had died as the result of a speeded-up blasting schedule that didn't allow adequate time for safety checks. He called it an unavoidable mishap because of the geology. Yet other people, including other engineers on the project, felt that the accident could have been prevented.

ACCIDENTS, LOST BUSINESS, AND THE RTC

A few years into construction of the subway, the atmosphere of excitement for this great undertaking had evaporated. The city was a mess. Its streets were in shambles, and dirt and dust were everywhere. Shops were losing business because customers couldn't get to them through the construction. The accidents were grievous and disheartening. People were very angry with the RTC. Belmont was the builder, but the public considered the RTC responsible for the mess.

When confronted with complaints about lost business or accidents, Parsons and the RTC brushed them aside. Businesspeople who complained were told that things would get better. And, luckily for everyone, the end of construction was in sight. The New York subway system was almost ready to open.

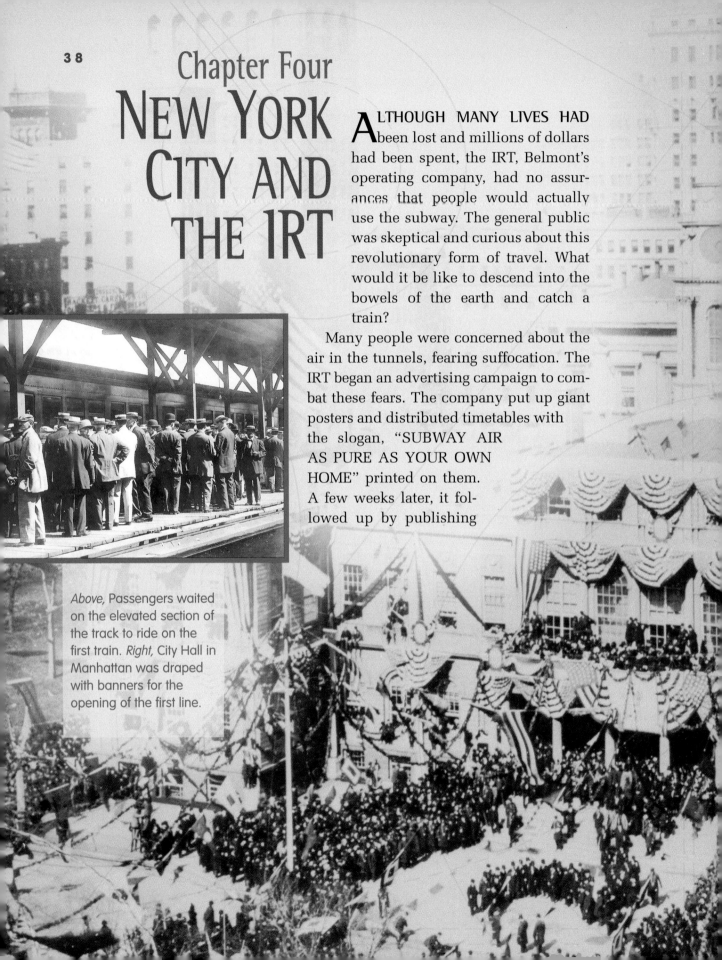

Chapter Four
NEW YORK CITY AND THE IRT

ALTHOUGH MANY LIVES HAD been lost and millions of dollars had been spent, the IRT, Belmont's operating company, had no assurances that people would actually use the subway. The general public was skeptical and curious about this revolutionary form of travel. What would it be like to descend into the bowels of the earth and catch a train?

Many people were concerned about the air in the tunnels, fearing suffocation. The IRT began an advertising campaign to combat these fears. The company put up giant posters and distributed timetables with the slogan, "SUBWAY AIR AS PURE AS YOUR OWN HOME" printed on them. A few weeks later, it followed up by publishing

Above, Passengers waited on the elevated section of the track to ride on the first train. *Right,* City Hall in Manhattan was draped with banners for the opening of the first line.

an impartial study by C. F. Chandler, a Columbia University professor, who reported the air in the underground subway tunnels was just as safe and healthy as the air above ground.

"TO HARLEM IN FIFTEEN MINUTES"

Then the IRT launched another campaign that emphasized the speed and convenience of the new transit system. In posters, leaflets, and public statements by IRT and city officials, the company began using the phrase "To Harlem in Fifteen Minutes." This slogan reminded people of the main advantage of subway travel: speed. On opening day, the slogan proved more than an idle boast when the first subway train made the trip in less than eleven minutes.

"I HEREBY DECLARE THE SUBWAY OPEN!"

The people of New York City were excited about their new subway. There was a carnival-like atmosphere in the city in the weeks before it opened. People held subway parties, and buildings were draped with banners.

On October 27, 1904, after more than four years of disruption, the first line of the subway was to open for business. It would still be a few months before the northern sections were finished, when riders would be able to travel from Manhattan to the Bronx in record time.

On the morning of October 27, the *New York Times* ran an article entitled "Subway Ifs and Don'ts." Using a question-and-answer format, the newspaper addressed such concerns as "Is subway travel injurious to the eyes?" and "What will happen if there is a fire in the subway?" They even printed a list of "Don'ts," such as, "Don't lower the top window unless you have to. The draughts are bad in the tunnel."

The official public opening was set for 7:00 P.M., but the whole day was packed with special events. Thousands of people gathered at City Hall to hear speeches honoring Belmont, Parsons, and McDonald. At 2:30 P.M., Mayor McClellan and a host of other dignitaries descended into the

MAYOR MCCLELLAN'S WILD RIDE

The first subway train that pulled away from the City Hall station on the afternoon of October 27, 1904, was full of dignitaries and politicians. Little did they know what they were in for. As the *New York Times* reported, "It was not part of the programme that Mayor McClellan *[below]* should act as motorman of the initial train. The mere starting of the machinery was to be his duty, . . ."

Mayor McClellan's job was ceremonial. He was supposed to start the train, then turn the controls over to a regular motorman. But the mayor was having so much fun that he refused to step aside. Despite pleas from E. M. Bryan and Frank Hedley, the IRT's vice president and general manager, respectively, McClellan stayed at the controls and increased the speed of the train.

As the train roared through tunnels and around curves, Hedley kept blasting the whistle to warn people they were coming down the track. At one point, McClellan accidentally hit the emergency brake, bringing the train to a screeching halt and sending the dignitaries flying through the air onto the hard wooden floor.

McClellan finally turned over the controls after the train had completed most of its run. He spent the rest of the trip with the other dignitaries. Puffing on a big cigar, he insisted that his "mastery" of the subway train was the result of knowing how to drive an automobile.

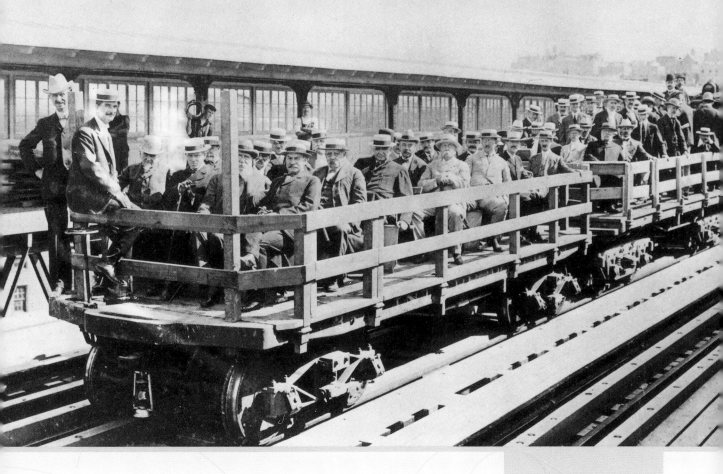

City Hall station and boarded a special train, officially opening the subway. It pulled away from the station with McClellan at the controls.

At the Manhattan Valley section of the route, the train traveled in the open on elevated tracks. People crowded onto fire escapes, swarmed onto rooftops, and congregated on the streets just to catch a glimpse of the first train. When the special train emerged from the tunnel, a cheer went up from the crowd, factories blew their sirens, and ships on the Hudson River tooted their whistles. The train slowed slightly and blew its whistle in response. The cheering and whistle blasts continued until the train reentered the tunnel and disappeared from sight.

At 7:00 P.M., the subway opened its doors to the public, and more than 110,000 people poured into the stations. Many couples celebrated by getting dressed up in their best clothes, going out to dinner,

Dignitaries in an open car had a pre-opening tour of the first subway. This photo was taken when they passed through Manhattan Valley on the elevated section of the line.

Passengers lined up at the oak and bronze ticket booths to pay their fares.

then going for a ride on the subway. Others bought their tickets and spent hours riding back and forth on the line. Some were so overwhelmed by the new surroundings, they stood in the stations gaping and never boarded a train.

Tickets to ride the subway were at a premium, as the *New York Times* reported. "The ticket agent received an offer of $25 for ticket No. 1, but he wouldn't take it. He bought the ticket himself for 3 cents. After that he received two or three offers of $40 for it, but he preferred to keep the ticket."

New Yorkers quickly adapted to the new mode of transportation. The very next day, October 28, the *New York Times* ran a feature article on the subway with the subhead: "An Old Story Even Now." But it still amazed people. On the same day, the *New York Times* also ran a story mentioning the behavior of different New Yorkers as they rode the train. "The up-bound Brooklynite . . . boarded the trains with [a] stolid air . . . unwilling to admit that anything surprised him. The Manhattanites boarded the train with the sneaking air of men who were ashamed to admit that they were doing something new, and attempting to cover up the disgraceful fact. They tried to cover it up with gibes and jokes."

Public excitement surrounding the new subway reached its peak two days later on Sunday, October 30. In 1904 most New Yorkers worked six days a week. Sunday was the only day they had for themselves. That Sunday nearly one million people tried to go "subway riding," as people called it. The lines to enter stretched for two blocks at one station. With only one route up and running, the IRT could handle only 350,000 passengers a day, so it was impossible for everyone to ride. As frustration levels rose, tempers grew short and fights broke out. The police had to be called in to restore order.

> "The Manhattanites boarded the train with the sneaking air of men who were ashamed to admit that they were doing something new, and attempting to cover up the disgraceful fact."
>
> —The *New York Times*
> October 28, 1904

Fears that New Yorkers wouldn't use the new subway appeared to be totally unfounded. New Yorkers loved the IRT. Within a week, newspapers were referring to the new phenomenon as "the subway crush." Trolleys and els had never experienced this kind of ridership.

ABOVE OR BELOW, SOME THINGS DON'T CHANGE

The first recorded theft on the subway occurred on the night the subway opened. Henry Barrett, a gentleman who had purchased the third ticket sold at the 28th Street station, boarded a subway train at 7:02 P.M. As he told police officers, he looked down at his jacket at 7:03 P.M. and discovered that his lapel pin with fifteen diamonds was gone.

A week after the subway opened, large advertising posters appeared

When the first advertising posters appeared in the subway stations, they were received with outraged protests.

on the walls of the stations. People were outraged as workers nailed enormous signs advertising Coke's Dandruff Cure and Baker's Cocoa onto the beautiful colored bricks. Both the Architectural League and the Municipal Art Society condemned the IRT and demanded the removal of the defacing signs. The public outcry against advertising was so strong that the municipal government of New York City even filed a lawsuit against the IRT to get the ads removed.

But the executives of the IRT had always planned to have advertising in the subway. They'd just never told the public about it. They had already signed agreements with several companies and stood to make more than $500,000 from the venture. They fought the lawsuit vigorously and eventually won. Advertising in the subway was there to stay.

CARS AND FARES

To New Yorkers, the subway was fascinating, even glamorous. The cars were brand new and much more luxurious than existing el or railroad cars.

Parsons had been considering designs for passenger cars even before Belmont signed the final contract. Purchasing and maintaining the cars was Belmont's responsibility, but the RTC controlled what type of cars were to be used. Ordinary railcars were too boxy to fit properly in the tunnels. The cars finally purchased for the new subway were lower and narrower than el cars, but 4 feet (1.2 m) longer. These original IRT cars had beautiful maple floors and mahogany

THE PROFITS
ARE IN THE STRAPS

The nickel fare was supposed to allow August Belmont to make a modest profit if the subway trains ran full, and all seats were occupied. But the more people who rode the subway—whether they had a seat or not—the more profit for Belmont and the IRT.

Within two months of its opening, the IRT was making a substantial profit. The subway cars were always crowded, especially during the morning and evening rush hours. People pushed and shoved into the cars, taking every available seat, then continued to push into the car until all standing space was also taken. Standees hung onto the straps suspended from the ceiling. This practice led the IRT's business staff members to coin the phrase: "The profits are in the straps."

Riders demanded more subways. But Belmont didn't want to spend the money to build other lines. He made the most money by packing the existing cars as full as possible.

There weren't any standees holding on to the leather straps in this subway car for ladies only.

EVERY NICKEL COUNTS

Within months of its opening, the IRT introduced a procedure designed to eliminate theft by employees, even if it was only a nickel at a time. Passengers bought a ticket at a booth manned by an employee. To enter the platform area and catch a train, they had to hand the ticket to another employee who tore it in half and deposited one half into a slot in a turnstile.

At the end of the day, people from the IRT's business office collected the ticket halves from the turnstiles and the nickels from the booths. Then they counted them to make sure they matched. If there were more ticket halves than nickels, they suspected the money-collecting employee of stealing.

woodwork with solid bronze fittings throughout. Each car had fifty-two seats—twenty-six seats on each side of a main aisle.

An added feature was two rows of leather hand straps, suspended from the ceiling on either side of the center aisle. People unable to get a seat could stand and hold on to the straps to keep their balance while the train was moving.

All this luxury was available to riders for a nickel fare. The ordinary working person could afford it, and Belmont still made a profit if the trains were full.

SPEED, SPEED, AND MORE SPEED

The thing New Yorkers liked best about the subway was its speed. Most of the IRT trains ran at close to 40 miles (65 km) per hour. By contrast, the trolley cars only went 6 miles (10 km) per hour, and the el traveled at 12 miles (19 km) per hour.

For some New Yorkers used to the speed of horse carts and trolleys, the subway turned out to be downright dangerous. Trolleys went so slowly, people scooted in front of them all the time. But people were often struck by subway trains when they tried to dash across the tracks because they had entered the station in the wrong direction.

Other people walked into the tunnels to explore the tracks. Some men took to using the subway tunnels as bathrooms. High-speed trains used these tunnels. They were no place to go walking or to answer the call of nature. So many people were struck and killed in the first month (including one man with his pants down) that the IRT was forced to issue warnings in the newspapers. The company put signs up saying: "ALL PERSONS ARE FORBIDDEN TO ENTER UPON OR CROSS THE TRACKS."

One guard mentioned a problem not found in the els or trolley cars. "Everything is running as smooth as silk," said one guard, who had long been in the employ of the elevated roads, "and there is only one trouble for us that I can see. We're going to be bothered with sleepers. As we whizz along the pillars come so fast that they give a foglike effect to folks who are looking out the windows. They half close their eyes and the next thing you know they are sound asleep."

TOO MANY PEOPLE, NOT ENOUGH SUBWAY

The four lines of the IRT were designed for no more than 600,000 passengers a day. The company had expected ridership to grow into that number over the course of several years. It was apparent almost immediately that the subways were woefully inadequate. A week after the first line opened, the *Real Estate Record and Builders Guide* announced that the subway should have been designed to handle much larger crowds. By October 1905, the IRT was already carrying its maximum passenger load. And by 1908, more than 800,000 people were packing into the subway every single day.

At a private party held the evening of the subway's opening day, John McDonald had stated in a speech, "It is now simply a question of more tunnels. There is not a street in the city that cannot be tunneled. . . . I think we have made the beginning of an underground city." By 1908 nearly everyone agreed that it was time to get on with the building of that underground city.

Chapter Five
MORE SUBWAYS FOR NEW YORK
(1905–1920)

ONLY TWELVE DAYS AFTER the opening of the IRT, August Belmont announced that he had no intention of building new subway lines to prevent crowding. They would take traffic away from the original lines and lower his profit. Because his contract with the RTC gave him control of the subway for fifty years, he could pretty much do what he wanted.

Belmont did open additional subway links to his original line in 1905 and 1906. These included a tunnel that went under the Harlem River to the Bronx and one into Brooklyn. Even with these additions, he continued to make huge profits, and the subway crush continued.

Between 1904, when the subway opened, and 1920, the population of Manhattan increased by 265 percent, a sharper rise than any other period of history. In 1910 2,333,542 people were living on the tiny 23-square-mile (60-square-km) island of

Subway use increased as the city's population grew between 1904 and 1920.

Manhattan, a greater population than that of thirty-three states combined. New York City was bursting at the seams. Population growth had rapidly outpaced the carrying capacity of the subway.

GOOD-BYE TO THE RTC

The RTC was more than willing to have other companies build and operate new subway lines. In March 1905, they had released a grandiose plan that included nineteen new lines stretching throughout every borough except Staten Island. This new plan called for additional subways to be linked to the IRT (thereby giving Belmont continued dominance of the subway system), as well as several separate lines that could be operated independently.

The estimated building cost of this new subway system was $250 million. But, given the phenomenal success of the IRT, the RTC was confident it could get a bidder for the new project.

After talking to several regional transit companies, the RTC found one, the Metropolitan Street Railway, that was willing to submit a bid. At the same time, the commission was talking with Belmont, trying to entice him to build the new lines that would connect to the IRT.

-SUBWAY-

The ideal situation would be for Belmont to agree to build the IRT connecting lines and for the Metropolitan to bid for the new routes. The subway crush would disappear, and the two companies could run their subways, each making a profit.

The IRT was an absolute gold mine for Belmont. He had no intention of being forced into building new lines that would dilute his profits or in letting other companies share the wealth. A few days before Christmas 1905, he eliminated his only subway rival by buying the Metropolitan Street Railway.

The public was stunned, but not nearly as stunned as the RTC. Instead of getting a new subway system from two companies fighting it out, it was now faced with one gigantic transportation company that refused to negotiate about anything. Unless the city was willing to build and operate the new lines, there would be no new subways.

The Progressives, a new group of reform politicians, advocated tighter government controls on public utilities and services. They didn't believe that the RTC, as it was set up, was capable of controlling Belmont or any other private company. Newspapers, encouraged by this reform group, immediately blamed the RTC for the contract that gave Belmont control of the subways. By January 1906, the papers were publicly calling for the abolition of the RTC. Fifteen months after the triumphant opening of the first subway, the RTC was in deep political trouble.

George McAneny worked out the Dual Contracts deal.

The Progressives managed to sweep into power that election year. By June 1907, the Rapid Transit Commission was no more. It had been abolished and replaced by a new agency—the Public Service Commission (PSC).

THE DUAL SYSTEM

Initially the PSC didn't fare much better than the RTC. Then, in 1911, the Brooklyn Rapid Transit Company (BRT) stepped forward with a workable offer. Perhaps most important, the BRT was already a huge transit company in Brooklyn. It was wealthy enough to assume the financial risk and take on

Belmont. The PSC, prompted by George McAneny, the Manhattan borough president, negotiated a deal with the BRT.

In the end, Belmont agreed to build and operate new subway lines, but his monopoly was broken. The IRT would be sharing the subway business with the BRT. This deal, hammered out by McAneny, was referred to as the Dual System or the Dual Contracts.

On March 19, 1913, officials of New York City, the IRT, and the BRT signed the contracts for a new subway system. The Dual Contracts contained an important clause that Belmont's original contract didn't have. It allowed the city to take over the subways at any time ten years after construction was completed. Unless the city agreed, no private company would be able to control the subway the way Belmont had controlled the IRT.

When completed, the Dual System would dwarf New York City's existing subways. Single-track mileage would more than double, increasing from 296 miles (476 km) of track to 619 miles (996 km) of track. The number of trains that moved in each direction would increase from 352 to 851 an hour.

TUNNELING

Both the BRT and the IRT were confident they could build the eight new tunnels that would carry the lines beneath the East River and the

A DUAL SYSTEM THAT WOULD NEVER MIX

The IRT and the BRT made sure their lines would never mix. The subway cars in each system were different. The BRT cars were modeled on actual railroad cars. The BRT wanted to connect its subway lines to its existing rail and el lines, so it used the same cars throughout the system. BRT cars were longer, wider, and boxier than the cars used by the IRT. The IRT's narrower, shorter cars fit the smaller IRT tunnels. The BRT cars couldn't get through them.

The handful of passageways that were built to connect the two systems were long, dirty, poorly lit, and designed only for pedestrians. Most passengers who needed to change from one line to the other had to take the stairs to street level, walk for several blocks, then descend into the other system.

The BRT and IRT refused to connect their lines. They both wanted to ensure that the other line didn't steal their passengers and profit.

Harlem River. The amount of underwater tunneling needed under the Dual Contracts was a distinguishing feature of the deal. When the IRT was first built, the lines stopped at the water. People got off, took a ferry, then caught another train. The building of the two underground tunnels in the original system had been plagued by accidents.

But by 1913, technology had improved. Drills and protective shields were stronger, dynamite was a bit more stable, and better safety regulations were in place.

Tunneling is always dangerous, but it's especially so with a river above. Atmospheric pressure is greater

Tunneling Underwater

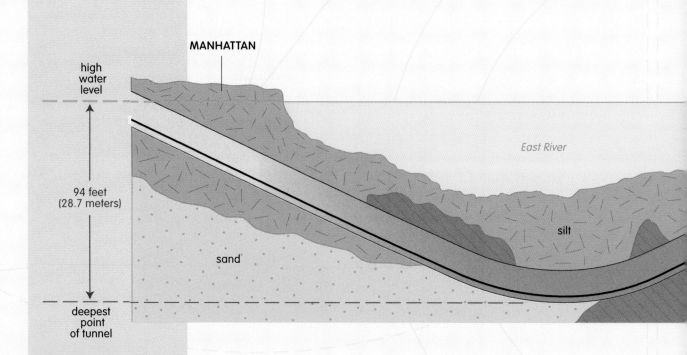

MANHATTAN

high water level

East River

94 feet
(28.7 meters)

silt

sand

deepest point of tunnel

underwater than on land, so the pressure in the underwater tunnel had to be controlled to make it safe for the sandhogs, as the workers who tunneled underwater are called.

Sandhogs entered the tunnel site by walking down four flights of stairs. They then trudged several hundred feet downhill in a narrow, muddy passage that ended under the river. There, they entered an air lock. This iron-walled room (similar to an elevator with doors on opposite sides) divided the zones of normal outside atmospheric pressure from the heavier pressure under the river.

The heavy doors of the air lock were closed. The chamber was gradually pumped full of compressed air until the workers became used to the increased pressure. When the atmospheric pressure in the air lock equaled the atmospheric pressure in the tunnel, the doors on the tunnel side of the chamber were opened and the workers exited.

Once the workers were safely under the river, the procedures were the same as for working in an aboveground tunnel. The workers drilled holes for dynamite, detonated the blasts, and hauled the debris away to the outskirts of the city. Everything took much longer, though, because of the need to go in and out of the air lock.

Accidents that occurred in the underwater tunnels turned out to be doubly dangerous. One minute the men would be drilling through the hard Manhattan schist. The next minute they'd hit a layer of broken rock or sand, and water would start pouring in. They not only risked being buried by a rock slide, but they also risked being drowned.

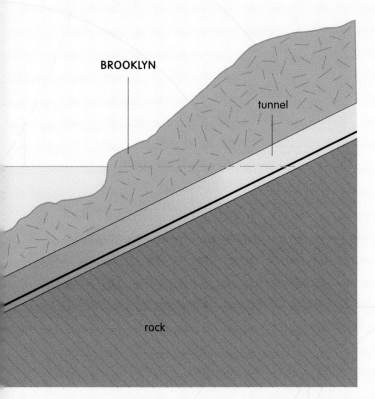

BROOKLYN

tunnel

rock

Sandhogs posed in the doorway of the air lock in a tunnel under the East River.

One time a tunnel under the East River blew out, killing two sandhogs. A third survived because the difference in air pressure sucked him out of the tunnel. The pressure pulled him through several feet of sand on the river bottom, then blasted him to the river's surface and 40 feet (12 m) into the air on a geyser of water. He managed to swim to a boat, where he was pulled from the river.

THE DUAL SYSTEM OPENS FOR BUSINESS

The BRT and the IRT finished most of the Dual System in the early 1920s. By that time, New Yorkers were accustomed to their gradually expanding subway, and very little fanfare marked its opening.

The New York subway system had become the largest in the world. Its routes totaled 201.8 miles (325 km), compared to 156.6 miles (252 km) in the London Underground, the next biggest system. If the tracks in the New York subway system had been laid end to end as a single track, they would have stretched from New York to Tennessee.

The carrying capacity of this expanded subway system was also staggering. In a single twenty four-hour period, it could carry thirty-five million people—one-third of the entire population in the United States at that time.

In a single day, New Yorkers could swim or ride the roller coaster at Coney Island in the morning, watch a baseball game in Yankee Stadium in the afternoon, then take in an evening movie at one of the theaters in Times Square. Each of these activities was in a different borough, but all of them were linked. The age of rapid transit had definitely arrived.

BLOWOUT

While digging for the IRT under the East River, a tunnel started to collapse. This caused the air lock to decompress—much like a deflating balloon. One sandhog, Dick Creedon, did exactly what he was supposed to do in that situation: he rushed to the collapsing site with a sandbag, ready to plug the leak. He was sucked through the hole, up through 30 feet (9 m) of riverbed and into the East River. Creedon was picked up by a tugboat, alive and swimming. The hole in the IRT tunnel was only repaired when boats delivered tons of sand to the location and dumped them into the water directly over the spot.

Chapter Six
THE IND AND UNIFICATION
(1920–1940)

THE 1920S AND 1930S WERE golden years for New Yorkers who needed inexpensive transportation. According to the terms of the original IRT contract and the newer Dual Contracts, the price for the subway was set at five cents. Then, as prices of everything else shot up, the nickel fare became the best bargain in town. Between 1904 and 1919, the price of a pound (0.45 kg) of coffee went from seven cents to twenty-two cents, girls' shoes went from $2.00 to $5.50, and the *New York Times* went from one to two cents a copy. In the 1920s, prices rose even higher.

While the nickel fare was great for the citizens of New York, it spelled doom for both subway

Above, New York mayor John Hylan was opposed to raising the five-cent fare. *Right,* In the 1920s, millions of subway passengers took advantage of this travel bargain.

companies. Steel (which subway cars were made of) went from $30.00 to $90.00 a ton (0.9 metric ton). A ton of coal (which the subway burned to produce its electrical power) went from $3.23 to $6.07. Even the price of brakes increased by 150 percent.

The subway had once been a gold mine for Belmont, but not any longer. With subway expenses rising rapidly and subway income stuck at the old rate, both the IRT and the BRT were on the verge of bankruptcy. Long after the fare should have been increased to cover operating costs, it remained set at a nickel, mostly due to the efforts of one man, Mayor John Hylan.

BAMBOOZLING THE PEOPLE

John Hylan was mayor of New York City from 1918 to 1925. He was convinced that any company could operate a subway on a nickel fare. Whenever the IRT or the BRT asked for a fare increase, Hylan blasted them on the front pages of the newspapers. He claimed that both subway companies were grasping, coldhearted corporations trying to bamboozle the people. Once he discovered that his popularity ratings went up with each attack, he never passed up an opportunity to criticize the subway companies and their fares.

Hylan made the five-cent fare a major campaign issue. He was convinced that the only way New York City would break free from the tyranny of the subway companies was to have a publicly owned subway that directly competed with the IRT and the BRT.

While most ordinary people sided with him on the fare issue, many businesspeople and politicians saw it differently. Some felt that a mass-transit system ought to be provided by the government with tax dollars, the same way roads, streetlights, water, and

JOHN HYLAN AND THE SUBWAY

John Hylan's ferocious hatred of the companies that ran the subway system stemmed from an incident that occurred long before he became mayor. Hylan had grown up poor on a farm in upstate New York, the oldest of five children. The family worked hard to make ends meet, and the children often went without shoes and other necessities. Because Hylan was always working, he never graduated from elementary school.

In 1887, at the age of nineteen, Hylan left home for New York City with only $3.50 in his pocket. On his first day in the city, he landed a job with the Brooklyn Union Elevated Railroad. Within two years, he had worked himself up to the position of locomotive engineer. Because he now earned $3.50 a day, he was able to get married, pay off the mortgage on his parents' farm, and support several of his siblings. He even went back to school for a law degree. For the next several years, he worked long hours, juggling work, school, and a clerkship in a law firm.

In September 1897, a month before graduating from law school, Hylan was driving his el train as usual one night. But after he rounded a curve, he nearly struck a company superintendent who was standing on the track. Although he denied all responsibility for the near-disaster, stating that the superintendent was a "very old man" who had stepped out from behind a switch tower without looking both ways, Hylan was instantly fired from his job. Luckily Hylan had some money saved. But it was still several years before he was on his feet financially again.

The Brooklyn Union Elevated Railroad was part of the BRT by the time Hylan became mayor. Although he publicly blasted both companies, he was always much harder on the BRT than on the IRT.

sanitation services were. No one expected those services to be profitable. There were even a few politicians who saw that the private subway companies could no longer be profitable. If New York City wanted a decent transit system, the city was probably going to have to pay for it.

Yet once Hylan made the five-cent fare an issue, no politician really dared speak out against it. Any politician who said, "The fare needs to be higher or the subway can't afford to run" or "We need to give the subway some tax monies" was considered to be on the side of the greedy corporations. Siding with the subway companies made it hard to get reelected.

During Hylan's first term in office, bills designed to help the struggling subways were introduced before the city council, but Hylan blocked all of them. The subway systems would receive no help from the city.

THE "PEOPLE'S SUBWAY"

Most of Hylan's time as mayor was spent trying to get approval for his new subway, one solely owned and operated by the city of New York. When he won a landslide victory in 1921, he declared, "My policy has been the preservation of democracy and the retention of the five-cent fare." On March 14, 1925, just before he left office, he got his wish. Wielding a silver pickax, Mayor Hylan removed the first chunk of dirt for the new Independent Subway System (IND). The "people's subway," as Mayor Hylan called it, would soon be a reality.

The IND system comprised 190 miles (306 km) of new tracks, spread out over seven lines. The first line opened in 1932, the last in 1940.

Construction of the IND lines began in 1925, and the first line opened in 1932.

THE MALBONE STREET STATION DISASTER

The worst disaster in the history of the New York subway system occurred during John Hylan's term as mayor. It involved a BRT train.

On November 1, 1918, the Brotherhood of Locomotive Engineers went on strike to protest the BRT's dismissal of twenty-nine motormen for trying to organize a union. In an effort to break the strike and to keep the trains running, clerks, administrators, supervisors, managers, and others found themselves running subway trains. Edward Luciano, a twenty-three-year-old dispatcher—someone who normally stayed in the office directing trains—was acting as a motorman.

Luciano, who had received only two and a half hours of training (not the normal twenty-one days), had never operated a subway train alone before. In addition to being exhausted by the emotional strain of the strike, Luciano was also recovering from the flu. This deadly epidemic had killed his child just the week before.

Luciano wanted to go home when his shift ended, but his supervisor insisted he take another run. Just before 7:00 P.M., Luciano's train roared down a steep hill toward the Malbone Street tunnel. The posted speed limit for that section of track was 6 miles (10 km) per hour. Yet eye witnesses swore the train was going 70 miles (113 km) per hour. Just before it entered the tunnel, the train derailed.

The first car plunged into the tunnel, and Luciano managed to escape with only some scrapes. But the next two wooden cars smashed against the concrete tunnel walls and were completely destroyed. As one newspaper reported, the "old wooden cars . . . crumbled like fruit cases when they struck the concrete wall of the Malbone Street tunnel." The sound of the crash was heard a mile away. Ninety-three people died in the Malbone crash, and Mayor Hylan publicly charged the BRT with "reckless disregard for human life."

The already struggling BRT went into bankruptcy on December 31, 1918. Five years later, when it had straightened out its financial affairs, it emerged under a new name, the Brooklyn-Manhattan Transit Corporation (BMT). The main reason the company changed its name was to distance itself from the Malbone disaster.

In 1919, one year after the accident, the name of the station was changed from Malbone Street to Empire Boulevard. The Malbone disaster remains the worst mass transit disaster in U.S. history.

The construction of the IND marked a dramatic change in the way New York laid out its rapid transit lines. Both the IRT and the BRT had expanded into new territory and were specifically designed to move people from congested areas to open outlying areas.

But the IND was built in downtown Manhattan, the center of New York City. It was designed to move people around already crowded areas. Most of its lines ran only a few blocks away from existing IRT and BRT lines, and all of its seven lines were constructed under streets using the cut-and-cover method. Only one tunnel was constructed beneath the East River.

The IND routes also ran underground beneath existing el routes. This was a deliberate decision on Hylan's part. If people had to choose between taking a subway or taking an el, they usually took the subway. The els, operated by the IRT and the BRT, were old, slow, and dirty. By building underground routes to compete with them, Hylan hoped to take business away from the IRT and the BRT. And just as Hylan had promised, the fare to ride anywhere on the IND was still five cents.

The IND lines ran below existing elevated routes to take business away from the els.

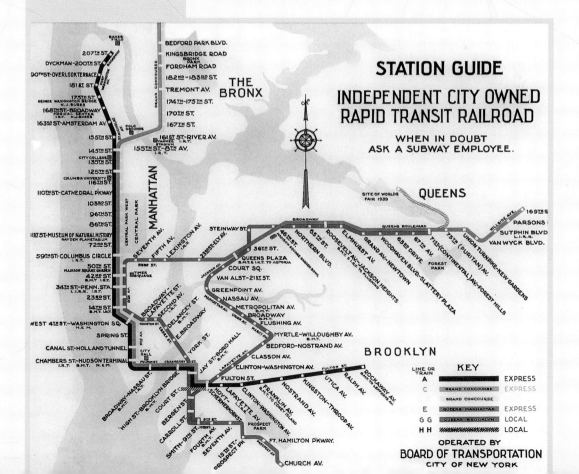

STILL NOT PROFITABLE

Even before the IND opened its first line, it was clear the nickel fare wouldn't begin to cover its operating costs. Hylan had his new subway for the people, but the IND was in financial trouble from the moment it opened. Fifteen years passed between the start of construction and the opening of all seven lines, partly because city officials, realizing the problem with the nickel fare, delayed as long as they could.

The entrances to the IND stations *(shown here in the 1960s)* weren't as elaborate as the early IRT kiosks.

Times had changed. When construction had begun on the first subway, the IRT, people were suspicious of government. Then public opinion shifted when the private business, controlled by Belmont, showed itself to be just as greedy and stubborn. At this point, the government stepped back in and excercised some control by working out the Dual Contracts with its option to take over the system after ten years.

In the 1920s, New York City was again growing by leaps and bounds. A rapid transit system was necessary to its economic health. People had to be able to get around the city. Other cities, such as London, Moscow, Prague, Berlin, and Paris, had quickly realized that

With the rise in the use of the automobile, transportation money went to highways and bridges, such as the George Washington Bridge, which crosses the Hudson River from Manhattan to New Jersey.

a cheap mass-transit system was vital to a large city's growth and survival. Without a good system, large cities would deteriorate into chaos. All these cities controlled their own subways and used tax monies to cover operating, maintenance, and expansion costs.

But New York's politicians didn't trust business, and business didn't trust politicians. Business could no longer run the subways profitably, and government wouldn't spend tax money on the subways.

THE DECLINE OF THE SUBWAY SYSTEM

The BRT declared bankruptcy in 1918, and the entire subway system was in decline in the late 1920s. Within the next ten years, the IRT entered into the legal stages of bankruptcy, too. Both companies remained in operation. The BRT even reorganized into a new corporation, the Brooklyn-Manhattan Transit Corporation, the BMT, but its financial matters were always shaky.

In an effort to save money and to keep the subway operating, both companies had cut their workforce in half. The whole system became dirty and unreliable. In the early 1920s, each ten-car subway train employed a motorman and five guards. By the mid-1930s, the same train used only a motorman and one guard. Maintenance crews were also cut back, so the trains ran slowly and broke down frequently. Garbage accumulated in all the stations.

MAYOR FIORELLO LAGUARDIA

Fiorello LaGuardia, *below,* was born in New York City in 1882, the son of recently arrived Italian immigrants. He spent most of his childhood on military bases because his father became a U.S. Army bandmaster shortly after LaGuardia was born. When his father was discharged in 1898, the family settled in Trieste, a town in modern-day Italy.

LaGuardia returned to New York City in 1906 and graduated from New York University's law school four years later. He was attracted to politics and quickly worked his way up through the Republican Party, serving as a congressman, then as president of the New York Board of Aldermen. He distinguished himself as a hardworking, incorruptible politician who refused to ally himself with any of the Tammany Hall bosses.

He was elected mayor of New York City in 1934, at one of the worst times in history. It was the depths of the Great Depression, and thousands were out of work. New York City had become a town of soup kitchens, breadlines, shantytowns, and closed banks. Small and stout, LaGuardia immediately took control of the situation, tackling every detail and refusing to delegate responsibility to anyone. As one person remarked, "It seemed as though the town had been invaded by an army of small plump men in big hats. He was everywhere."

LaGuardia was not particularly interested in transit. He preferred to spend his time creating employment and helping banks get back on their feet. But he realized that the subway system was in big trouble. The mayor was determined to keep the five-cent fare, reorganize the subways, and create a government agency to manage them. By the end of his term, he had done all these things. LaGuardia is remembered as one of the greatest mayors New York City has ever had.

The subway was also facing stiff competition from the automobile. In 1920 there were only 9 million registered automobiles in the United States. In 1925 there were 20 million. The automobile was able to open up new territories and to move people out of the city more easily than the subway. Tax monies that might have gone to the subways went toward the construction of highways and bridges.

In the mid-1930s, the New York subway system (all three companies) was on the verge of total economic collapse. Like it or not, something had to be done. If three separate subway systems couldn't make money, perhaps one unified system could.

UNIFICATION

The potential had existed for the city to take over operation of the subways even before the signing of the Dual Contracts. Although Belmont's original contract for the IRT granted him almost exclusive ownership of the line, there was still the clause that limited these rights to fifty years.

In 1934, when Fiorello LaGuardia was elected mayor of New York City, he began efforts to unify the IRT, the BMT, and the IND into one city-owned system. In 1940, after much haggling, the city of New York purchased both the IRT and the BMT and, with the IND, reorganized them into one subway system.

At 11:55 P.M., on May 31, 1940, the last BMT train made its way through the tunnels. At midnight ownership of the company transferred to New York City. And at midnight, June 12, 1940, the IRT transferred everything to the city. Private operation of the New York subway system had become a thing of the past.

The merger of the IRT, the BMT, and the IND into one city-owned system was the largest railroad merger in the history of the United States. With a purchase price of more than $329 million, the merger was also the biggest financial transaction the city had ever undertaken. Signing the checks and the transfer papers took more than four hours.

To manage the unified subway system, a new city agency was formed, the New York City Transit System (NYCTS). The NYCTS controlled all forms of public transportation, including 760 miles (1,223 km) of subway and el tracks, 435 miles (700 km) of street railways, and 80 miles (129 km) of bus lines. It was the largest transit system in the world. It was also the most heavily used. In NYCTS's first year of operation, 2.3 billion passengers used the system. About 1.8 billion were subway passengers.

The subway system was a vital part of New York City. The city couldn't afford to let it deteriorate. Everyone hoped unification would solve the financial problems.

Chapter Seven
INTO THE FUTURE WITH THE MTA

(1940–present)

BY 1940 THE NEW YORK SUB-ways had become a unified system. Fiorello LaGuardia was mayor, the Great Depression was ending, and subway ridership was soaring. All appeared to be well. New Yorkers were riding their subway as never before. From its lowest point of 1.7 billion passengers in 1933, subway ridership rose to more than 2 billion in 1947.

Things looked good, but the figures were misleading. The NYCTS was in trouble. People were riding the subway system because public transportation was the only way to get around. World War II (1939–1945) began during LaGuardia's terms

Subway cars and stations were jammed with passengers when ridership grew to more than 2 billion in 1947.

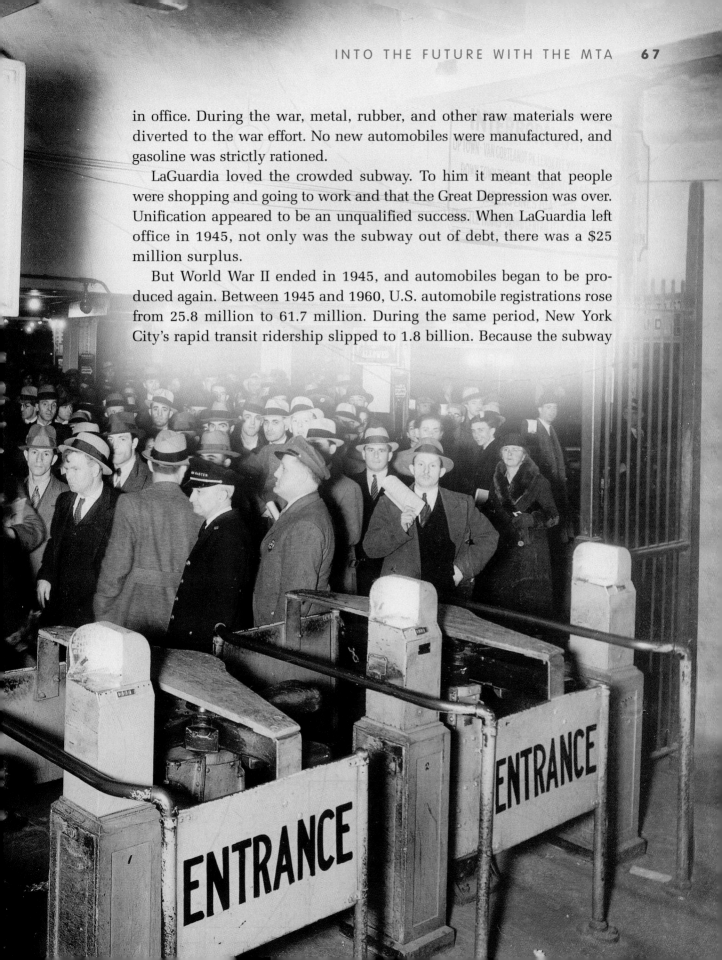

in office. During the war, metal, rubber, and other raw materials were diverted to the war effort. No new automobiles were manufactured, and gasoline was strictly rationed.

LaGuardia loved the crowded subway. To him it meant that people were shopping and going to work and that the Great Depression was over. Unification appeared to be an unqualified success. When LaGuardia left office in 1945, not only was the subway out of debt, there was a $25 million surplus.

But World War II ended in 1945, and automobiles began to be produced again. Between 1945 and 1960, U.S. automobile registrations rose from 25.8 million to 61.7 million. During the same period, New York City's rapid transit ridership slipped to 1.8 billion. Because the subway

ENTRANCE   ENTRANCE

depended on the income from fares to pay its operating costs, the loss of passengers put an enormous financial strain on the city of New York.

THE END OF THE NICKEL FARE

The nickel fare had held steady since the first subway opened in 1904. By the 1940s, New York City had the only subway system in the world that had not raised its fare.

The city and the NYCTS took over the management of the transit system with optimistic plans. They watched with dismay as the subway continued to lose money. When Belmont and private corporations had run it, the public—and politicians—had blamed any problems on corporate greed. But problems were now the fault of New York City's elected politicians. Mayor William O'Dwyer wanted to raise the fare, but he needed to get at least one prominent group to support the move.

In 1948 the head of the Transit Workers Union (TWU), Mike Quill, had discussions with the mayor. Quill announced that he and the TWU would support a fare increase to ten cents. New York City's transit system employed more than thirty-five thousand workers. The transit workers saw a fare increase as the first step toward a wage increase. With the backing of the transit workers, Mayor O'Dwyer announced that, effective July 1, 1948, the subway and el fares would increase to ten cents. Streetcar and bus fares would rise to seven cents.

Since that first fare raise, subway fares have increased more than a dozen times. In the early 2000s, New Yorkers paid $1.50 per ride.

In 1953 tokens replaced coins so that the coin-operated entryways wouldn't have to be changed each time the fare was raised.

THE END OF THE NYCTS

Even after several fare increases, the subway was still losing money. People began looking for yet another solution to the problem. Just as the Rapid Transit Commission had been abolished in 1907 in favor of the Public Service Commission, the NYCTS also came under attack.

TICKETS, TOKENS, AND METROCARDS

Subway fares have taken many forms over the years. From paper tickets, to metal tokens, to the MetroCard, subway administrators are always looking for a better way to collect the fare.

When the IRT first opened in 1904, passengers purchased a paper ticket for a nickel, then presented the ticket to a "ticket chopper," another employee, who tore it in half. But in 1920, in an effort to save money, Belmont installed automatic turnstiles (entryways) in the subway. Passengers dropped their nickel directly into the turnstile, which then released and admitted them onto the platform. Hundreds of ticket choppers were fired when automatic turnstiles were installed.

Turnstiles that accepted coins were used until 1953. Shortly after its formation, the New York City Transit Authority (NYCTA) modified the turnstiles to accept tokens. Turnstiles that only accepted coins had to be altered to accept different coins every time the fare changed. By switching to tokens, passengers just paid more money for each token when the fare increased, but the turnstile didn't need to be altered.

Halved tickets worked well to control theft, and so did tokens. But tokens are extremely cumbersome. In 2001 more than four million people rode the New York subway everyday. If they all used tokens, and if the tokens from one single day's use were stacked in a tower, they would reach more than 33,000 feet (10,000 m) into the air—as high as most jets fly.

In 1997 NYCTA'S replacement, the Metropolitan Transit Authority (MTA) added MetroCards as another option. MetroCards look like credit cards, and passengers can buy them from the token clerk or from a machine. MetroCards come in single or multiple ride amounts. They can be used on city buses and for tranfers between the subway and buses. Sometime in the future, MetroCards will be the only way to enter the subway platform.

In 1953 the NYCTS was abolished and replaced with a new governing agency, the New York City Transit Authority (NYCTA). The NYCTA was set up to lease the subway from the city for a period of ten years and to run it as a private corporation. This tactic was supposed to separate the subway from city government, so its losses wouldn't show up in the city's budget.

The NYCTA was abolished in 1968 in favor of yet another agency, the Metropolitan Transit Authority (MTA). But no administrative maneuvering or political changes could stop the subway from deteriorating.

In the 1970s and 1980s, city government had little money for subway maintenance, and graffiti covered most subway cars.

CRIME AND THE SUBWAY

The subways continued to deteriorate. Beginning in the 1960s, serious crimes, including murder, were

GHOST STATIONS

The New York subway system has been expanding since construction first began. But even as lines are added, some stations close. These abandoned stations are called ghost stations.

New York's subway system has more than twenty ghost stations. Some are completely closed off, located on lines no longer used, with no trains ever passing them. Others can be briefly glimpsed through the windows of a modern subway car as it roars past the abandoned platforms. Still others have been abandoned as stations but are being used as storage facilities. The Court Street station, closed in 1946, houses New York City's Transit Museum.

Stations are usually closed because of poor ridership or close proximity to another, more heavily used station. Sometimes they're closed for safety reasons. The City Hall station was the most magnificent station in the New York subway system. Boasting ornate arches, colored glass tilework, skylights, and brass chandeliers, the station was the pride of the system. But when longer cars with center doors were introduced in the early 1940s, the tight curve at the City Hall station made it dangerous to open the doors. The station was closed in 1945. Occasionally the Transit Museum offers tours of the station and hopes to open it to the public someday.

Nearly every subway system in the world has ghost stations. The Paris Metro has eleven, while the London Underground has nearly forty. The Toronto subway system has put one of its ghost stations to good use, renting it out to movie companies for filming. Most ghost stations remain ghostly, glimpsed only as a pale flash from the windows of a speeding train.

being committed in subway trains and at stations in alarming numbers. By the 1980s, the subway had become a symbol of all that was wrong with urban America—filth, graffiti, and crime prevailed.

There was no money for repairs or maintenance. In 1964 subway cars traveled 34,294 miles (55,179 km) before a breakdown. But by 1984, they were traveling only 9,000 miles (14,500 km) before breaking down.

Beginning in the 1960s, crime and frequent breakdowns drove down subway ridership. Renovations began in the 1980s.

A MODERN SYSTEM

In 1982 the city, state, and federal government dedicated roughly $24 billion toward the New York City transit system. This funding increased regularly. By 2000 nearly all of the New York transit system was in excellent condition. Stations had been renovated, lines had been repaired, reliable trains had been added, and service had been increased.

In 1995 the New York City Police and the Transit Police Departments merged into a single unit. The part of the police force that patrols the New York subway system is the fifth largest police force in the United States.

This massive investment in funds and personnel has paid off. In 2001, for the first time since World War II, the growth in subway ridership outstripped the growth in auto use in all five of New York City's boroughs. Officials attributed this growth to New York's booming economy, the convenience of the MetroCard, a sharp drop in the crime rate, and a large increase in immigration. The New York City transit system carries 1.2 billion passengers every year—more than the yearly ridership of the transit systems of Boston, Chicago, Los Angeles, Philadelphia, and Washington, D.C., combined.

The New York City subway system is roughly one hundred years old. After decades of neglect, it appears to be moving into the future with New York City. Officials are quick to acknowledge that the system must continue to improve and expand to keep pace with the city's population. Because the last renovation program was so successful, the government of New York City intends to keep the subway funded to keep this great building feat a working, vital part of New York City.

THE BOMBING OF THE WORLD TRADE CENTER

On September 11, 2001, terrorists hijacked two passenger planes and crashed them into the twin towers of the World Trade Center in lower Manhattan. The buildings collapsed, causing the loss of thousands of lives. The subway tunnels under the World Trade Center, *below,* were crushed by the falling buildings. Steel beams were bent like paper clips, ceilings gave way, and building rubble filled the tunnels. As the World Trade Center site was cleared, plans were made to rebuild the subways underneath. More than one mile (1.6 km) of subway tunnel, floor, ceiling, and walls will be rebuilt, and new signal and transportation systems will be installed. New York city planners would like to rebuild the destroyed lines. They'd also like to modernize the maze of subway tunnels and connections that the competing IRT, BRT, and IND lines created in the early twentieth century.

A Timeline of the New York Subways

1863   The London Underground opens.

1867   Charles Harvey builds elevated West Side & Yonkers Patent Railway.

1870   Alfred E. Beach's pneumatic subway opens.

1888   Mayor Abram Hewitt proposes New York subway system.

1900   August Belmont signs contract to build first New York subway line. Groundbreaking ceremony for the IRT line takes place.

1904   Grand opening of the the IRT line

1905–1906   Belmont adds additional miles to the IRT.

1913   City signs Dual Contracts with the IRT and the BRT.

1918   Malbone Street station disaster

1925 Mayor John Hyland breaks ground for city-owned subway.

1940 Privately operated subway lines taken over by New York City.

May 31, 1940 Last run of the BMT

June 12, 1940 Last run of the IRT

1948 End of nickel fare. Fare increases to ten cents.

1982 $24 million is dedicated to restoring subway system.

1995 New York City and Transit Police Departments merge.

1997 Metrocard is introduced.

2001 Subway lines under World Trade Center buried in towers' collapse.

Source Notes

Acknowledgments for quoted material: p. 8, as quoted in Brian Cudahy, *Under the Sidewalks of New York* (New York: Fordham University Press, 1995); p. 12, as quoted in *The New York Subway: Its Construction and Equipment.* Reprinted on the web at <http://www.nycsubway.org/irt/irtbook/>; pp. 19, 33, 42–43, 43 (bottom), 45, 58, 59 (both), 63 (both), 64, as quoted in Clifton Hood, *722 Miles: The Building of the Subways and How They Transformed New York.* (Baltimore: Johns Hopkins University Press, 1993); p. 34, Framberger, "Architectural Designs for New York's First Subway," Historic American Engineering Record, National Park Service, Department of the Interior, Washington, D.C., <http://www.nycsubway.org/irtaer/architectural-design.html>; pp. 38, 39, 47, as quoted in Tim McNeese, *The New York Subway System* (San Diego: Lucent Books, 1997); p. 40 (top), "Some Subway Ifs and Don'ts," *New York Times*, October 27, 1904. Reprinted on the web at <http://www.nycsubway.org/irt>; p. 40 (bottom), "McClellan Motorman of First Subway Train," *New York Times*, October 28, 1904. Reprinted on the web at <http://www.nycsubway.org/irt>; p. 42, "Our Subway Open: 150,000 Try It," *New York Times*, October 28, 1904. Reprinted on the web at <http://www.nycsubway.org/irt>; p. 47, "Things Seen and Heard Along the Underground," *New York Times*, October 28, 1904. Reprinted on the web at <http://www.nycsubway.org/irt>.

Selected Bibliography

Bohlen, Celestine. "The Old World Under the New." *New York Times,* August 18, 2001, A17.

Brennan, Joseph. *Abandoned Stations.* 2001. <http://www.columbia.edu/~brennan/abandoned> (Summer 2002).

"The Capital Program," New York City Transit. 2001. <http://www.mta.nyc.ny.us/nyct/facts/ffcap.htm> (Summer 2002).

Cudahy, Brian J. *Under the Sidewalks of New York: The Story of the World's Greatest Subway System.* New York: Fordham University Press, 1995.

Encyclopedia Britannica. "Tammany Hall." 2001. <http://www.britannica.com> (Summer 2002).

Hood, Clifton. *722 Miles: The Building of the Subways and How They Transformed New York.* Baltimore: Johns Hopkins University Press, 1993.

Interborough Rapid Transit Company. *The New York Subway: Its Construction and Equipment.* Reprinted at <http://www.nycsubway.org.irt/irtbook>

Kennedy, Randy. "Transit Outpaces Cars, Study Finds," *New York Times,* August 8, 2001, A19.

Metropolitan Transit Authority. <http://www.mta.nyc.us/> (Summer 2002).

The New York City Subway. <http://www.nycsubway.org> (Summer 2002).

"New York City Transit History," New York City Transit. 2001. <http://www.mta.nyc.ny.us/nyct/facts/ffhist.htm> (Summer 2002).

Williams, Hywel. *London Underground History—Disused Stations.* 2001. <http://www.starfury.demon.co.uk/uground/> (Summer 2002).

Further Reading and Websites

Gelman, Amy. *New York*. Minneapolis: Lerner Publications Company, 2002.
Learn more about New York City and the rest of New York State.

"The IRT Division." *The New York City Subway.*
<http://www.nycsubway.org/irt/index.html>
This website includes a wealth of information on the Interborough Rapid Transit Company, New York City's first subway company. It includes an entire book published in 1904 on the subway's construction, a collection of newspaper articles from the subway's "Day One," and plenty of images of the old subway.

McNeese, Tim. *The New York Subway System*. San Diego: Lucent Books, 1997.
This book for junior high readers chronicles the history of the New York subway system from its construction to the mid-1950s.

"Subway Trains." *Forgotten New York.*
<http://www.forgottenny.com/SUBWAYS/Subways%20homepage/subways.html>
Discover the remains of an older New York City amidst the new in this collection of photos and information about subway trains, tracks, signs, and stations.

Wright, Susan. *New York City in Photographs,* 1850–1945. New York: Barnes & Noble Books, 1999.
Witness a century of tremendous change in New York City, from the Civil War to World War I in this book for advanced readers.

Index

Lesley A. DuTemple has written more than a dozen books for young readers, including many award-winning titles such as her biography *Jacques Cousteau,* winner of the National Science Teachers Association/Children's Book Council Outstanding Science Trade Books for Children. After graduating from the University of California, San Diego, she attended the University of Utah's Graduate School of Architecture, where she concentrated in design and architectural history. The creator of the **Great Building Feats** series, she believes, "There's a human story behind every one of these building feats, and those stories are just as amazing as the projects themselves."

Photo Acknowledgments

The images in this book are used with the permission of: New York Transit Museum Archives, Brooklyn, pp. 1, 6, 21, 41, 44, 54, 61; © Museum of the City of New York, pp. 2–3, 16–17, 32, 35, 59; © Frances M. Roberts, p. 4; © Richard B. Levine, pp. 4–5; Library of Congress (LC-USZC4-4637), pp. 8–9; © Brown Brothers, pp. 10, 11, 18, 19, 22, 26, 27, 28, 31, 36, 38, 40, 42, 45, 48–49, 50, 56, 56–57, 62, 63, 64, 66–67, 72; © Hulton Archive, p. 15; © Collection of The New-York Historical Society, neg. #37851 pp. 24–25; © Bettman/CORBIS, pp. 38–39; © Todd Strand/Independent Picture Service, pp. 68, 69; © Jerry Cooke/CORBIS, p. 70; © AP/Wide World Photos, p. 73; U.S. Department of the Interior Geological Survey, pp. 74–75. Maps and diagrams by Laura Westlund, pp. 13, 30, 52–53.

Cover photos are by © Underwood & Underwood/CORBIS (front), © Brown Brothers (back), and U.S. Department of the Interior Geological Survey (background).